BetterAt /School

A platform for student-centered mobile learning

IIT Institute of Design Publications
ISBN 9780615874876

This work is licensed under the Creative Commons Attribution-NonCommercial-NoDerivs 3.0 Unported License. To view a copy of this license, visit http://creativecommons.org/licenses/by-nc-nd/3.0/.

FOR MORE INFORMATION

http://www.better.at
More about BetterAt/School and other BetterAt projects.

http://www.id.iit.edu
More about Institute of Design and other research projects.

http://www.gatesfoundation.org
More about Bill & Melinda Gates Foundation projects related to learning.

http://www.macfound.org
More about John D. and Catherine T. MacArthur Foundation projects related to digital media and learning.

BetterAt/School is a project supported by The Bill & Melinda Gates Foundation. The goal of the project is to explore ways that interest based learning software might bridge the gap between the Common Core Standards and the lack of motivation frequently found in low-income students.

This project builds upon research begun in 2005 at IIT Institute of Design (ID) funded by the John D. and Catherine T. MacArthur Foundation. This work centered on identifying ways that digital media could be beneficial to interest based learning. One of the initiatives that emerged from that was the Electronic Learning Record, which quickly developed into BetterAt.

A core assumption of this work is that learning is enhanced when it relates to a student's goals and interests. For kids from home environments where they see a variety of jobs and people with choices about their future, the standard school experience can be supportive. For kids without these examples and choices, digital media can help by letting them start with their existing interests to expand their view of possible options.

The initial challenge for the Gates project was to find ways to relate intrinsic interests to the Common Core, with the ultimate goal of helping students prepare for college and productive careers.

We thank the Bill & Melinda Gates Foundation and the John D. and Catherine T. MacArthur Foundation for their support of research at Institute of Design.

SPRING 2013

Background, Context, Objectives
A design approach to the problem of low student engagement

Looking around some public high schools, it can be difficult to recognize how very different they are today than they were a hundred years ago. Classrooms are still organized for thirty students in a single grade to sit quietly and listen to lectures or work independently for forty or so minutes per period. Schools still sit empty between early June and Labor day for reasons most people don't remember. And students still move through grades as if on an invisible assembly line, with most—just over three-quarters of students[1]—graduating within four years. For many students—those with ample family resources—this model works well enough. But for many others—mostly low-income minority students—the model fails.

The data are easy to find, the symptoms are recognizable, and the core drivers are well-understood. The National Center for Education Statistics reports that 33.9% of African-American students and 28.6% of Hispanic students fail to graduate within four years.[2] Many of these students are concentrated in struggling schools. A recent study reveals that 25% of all African-American students and 17% of Hispanic students attend a school where fewer than 60% of students graduate in four years.[3] Student disengagement, chronic absenteeism, and boredom are visible signs that school is increasingly irrelevant for these students.

What is difficult is figuring out what to do about it. One approach is to address the problem with a system-centered point of view. A system-centered approach focuses on the design of new subsystems (such as assessments and curriculum standards) to improve or optimize a problematic aspect of the existing system. This approach has the advantage of attacking the problem at scale, with the possibility of improving conditions for a significant number of people. The downside is that this approach is often cumbersome, inflexible, and slow in development. Teachers and administrators frequently struggle to adapt these new subsystems to their own school environments, which slows adoption of even a valuable system innovation. And the rapid pace of change in the school environment means that some system innovations quickly lose impact as the conditions for which they were optimized evolve or erode in unforeseen ways.

An alternative is to design for the parts of the system that are beyond hierarchical control—in other words, to take a *human-centered* design approach. A key advantage of human-centered design is that its methodology is optimized for rapidly changing contexts and loosely defined problems with ambiguous boundaries, such as are often found in schools. By relying on direct observation and abductive logic, designers can quickly develop fresh insights and solutions and integrate temporal considerations into design strategy.

The core principle behind human-centered design is to empower the people most affected by the problem to solve the problem in ways that make most sense to them. This approach often results in the design of platforms—modular assemblies of solutions that users can combine in different ways to address a wide array of issues. Such flexibility can be an important driver of user adoption. The downside is that human-centered solutions can be difficult to scale.

In reality, the two approaches need not be mutually exclusive. It can be fruitful to combine the two approaches to exploit the advantages and mitigate the undesirable characteristics of each. The primary purpose of this research was to add a human-centered design approach to an existing system-centered solution—the Common Core State Standards (CCSS) to address the problem of low student engagement.

Students in a New York City classroom, 1913.

The computer lab in a Chicago classroom, 2011.

New Technology, Old Ways of Learning

The persistence of the industrial model

Digital technology has changed the way many people think about learning. But schools have been slow to adapt, often for completely logical reasons. Outmoded physical plants, the high cost of new infrastructure, administrators' reliance on existing systems, and concerns about the safety of users and the privacy of data all combine to constrain a school's ability to take full advantage of new technology. Instead of driving innovation, the adoption of new educational technology today often means simply automating old methods.

Contents

The Platform
A modular assembly of solutions to address low engagement **8**

Part 1 Learning

Today, teens have unprecedented access to the latest technology—but waning interest in school **9**

RESEARCH FINDINGS
The Experience Divide
In many schools today, standards don't simply drive the curriculum, they *are* the curriculum **12**

EXAMPLES
Alicia is Struggling to Find Her Path
A school with low scores—a girl with high hopes **17**

Ahmed Learns by Doing and Thinks by Making
This is what high-performance learning looks like **18**

CONCEPTS
Expert Challenges
Engaging students by engaging the real world **20**

The Civic Learning Network
Moving learning from an institution-centered approach to a kid-centered approach **24**

The Expert Network
Connecting kids directly to professional expertise **26**

Learning Design Services
Supporting change, creating content **27**

Part 2 Teaching

For today's teachers, student engagement and academic rigor are competing objectives 27

RESEARCH FINDINGS
Teaching Models
Curriculum-driven, interest-driven, or project-driven—the landscape of teaching 30

How Kids Discover Interests
Moving from confusion, serendipity, and discovery to realization 32

Interest-Based Learning in Formal Learning Contexts
From delivering content to setting the conditions for learning 24

The Literacy Design Collaborative Instructional Standards, The Common Core, and BetterAt/School
Building blocks for a new modular system 36

EXAMPLE
Delia Feels the Pressure of Standardized Testing
For teachers like Delia, backward planning is just backward 39

CONCEPTS
Starter Plans
Mixing and remixing great learning ideas—without losing rigor 40

The BetterAt/School Activity Framework
Providing students a design-driven process for real-world problem solving 44

Part 3 Assessing

Assessing what students know is easy. Assessing how they learned it is much more difficult 45

RESEARCH FINDINGS
Process Assessment
Making the learning process seamless from end to end 48

EXAMPLE
Paul Wants to See How Students Apply What They Are Learning
Teachers like Paul understand that students possess capabilities that can't be measured on standardized tests 50

CONCEPT
The BetterAt/School Interface
Making the student learning process visible 52

Appendix

THE DESIGN PROCESS
Sense Intent 56
Know Context and Know People 58
Frame insights 66
Explore Concepts and Frame Solutions 68
Realize Offerings 72

THE RESEARCH PLAN
Research Areas, Research Questions, Design Principles 74
BetterAt/School Team, Student Contributors 75
Participating Schools, and Youth Organizations 76
References 77

The Platform
A moduar assembly of solutions to address low engagement

BetterAt/School is a mobile learning platform with a set of protocols designed to optimize its use in formal learning contexts such as schools. In addition to the core web interface, BetterAt/School includes mobile apps, content, and learning design services. The modular components of the BetterAt/School platform can be combined in a variety of ways to serve different sets of user needs.

WEB INTERFACE

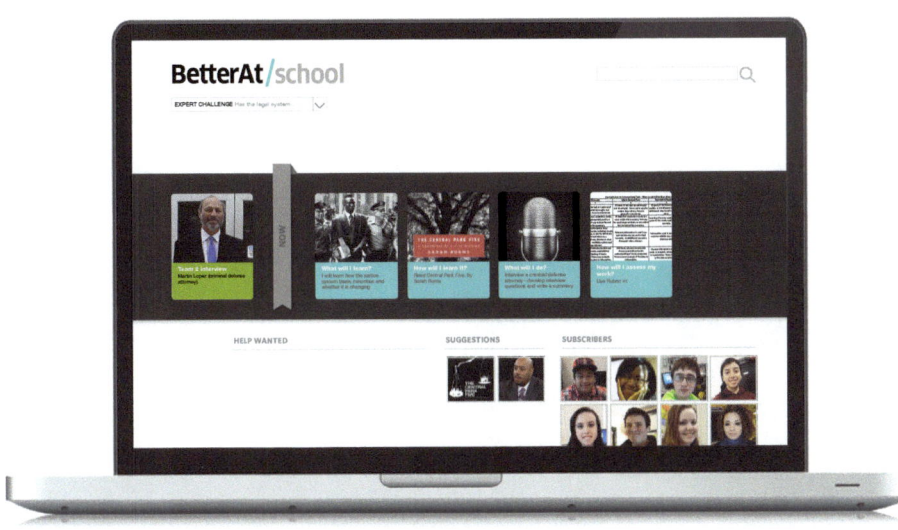

BETTERAT/SCHOOL TIMELINE
Page 49

MOBILE APPS

BETTERAT/SCHOOL iPAD APP
Page 51

BETTERAT/SCHOOL iPHONE APPS
Pages 40, 52

SERVICES	CONTENT
CIVIC LEARNING NETWORK *Pages 22–23*	**EXPERT CHALLENGES** *Pages 18–19*
Expert Network *Page 24* / **Learning Design Services** *Page 25*	**STARTER PLANS** *Pages 38–39*
	The Instructional Framework *Page 20* / **The Activity Framework** *Pages 42–43*

PART 1 LEARNING

Today, teens have unprecedented access to the latest technology—but waning interest in school

According to the Pew Internet and American Life Project, more than three-quarters of all teens age 12 to 17 have cellphones. A quarter of those have smart phones. Teens who have smart phones increasingly use their phones, not a computer, to access the Internet. Teens now spend more time on their cellphones, tablets, and computers than they spend in their classrooms.[4]

Digital communications technology has been liberating to teens. They are almost never out of contact with their social networks and spend hours online indulging their curiosity. Teens can now explore whatever topic they want, in whatever way they want, whenever they want—except in school.

At the same time, almost half of all high school students report feeling unengaged (present but not involved with or enthusiastic) when in school. Over a quarter of those unengaged students report being actively disengaged—in other words, they behave in ways that undermine their own and others' educational process.[5] Every year, many of these disengaged kids will join the 30% of American high school students who, for whatever reason, drop out of school.

"My students, unlike middle-class students in other parts of Chicago, do not meet many adults with careers and because of that, they don't realize the options available to them. Because of the poverty and gang violence, my students often have little freedom to leave their neighborhoods, participate in activities after school, and discover other options."—*Bill, instructional guide*

RESEARCH FINDINGS

The Experience Divide

In many schools today, standards don't just drive the curriculum, they are the curriculum

The trend is well established, persistent, and distressing. The achievement gap between low-income minority kids and their more affluent white peers is significant and growing. One way to understand this trend is to view it through the lens of student experience—to compare the school experiences of low-income minority students with the school experiences of more affluent students.

STUDENTS IN LOW-INCOME COMMUNITIES
Students in low-income communities, in schools that struggle with low student achievement, often encounter an educational culture that is overwhelmingly standards-focused. Limited school resources frequently drive school leaders to narrow the curriculum to only those subjects covered by standardized tests. Art, music, drama, and other subjects that might capture a student's interest and nurture his or her talents get little, if any, investment. Instructional time gets cut to make way for intensive test preparation. Often with little support from the community, and faced with concerns about students' and teachers' personal safety, school becomes more and more isolated from the real world. As the years tick by, students find it increasingly difficult to imagine themselves in college or a career as school becomes increasingly irrelevant to their lived experience.

STUDENTS IN AFFLUENT COMMUNITIES
Students in affluent schools most often encounter a culture focused on college and career. These students are surrounded by highly educated people working as professionals, managers, skilled technicians, or entrepreneurs. While also standards-based, the curriculum in affluent schools is wide ranging, integrating the interests of faculty and the student body, and centered on developing curiosity and inquiry among students. After-school activities extend knowledge covered in the classroom, often by giving students a chance to apply what they've learned to something they care about in real life. Affluent students find it easy to imagine themselves in college and careers because everything in their learning environment—the mentoring they receive, the learning experiences their teachers create for them, and the family and social connections that provide them glimpses

The Experience Divide

Students in low-income schools tend to encounter a basic curriculum heavily focused upon standards-based instruction, while students in more affluent schools encounter a curriculum that is based on standards, but focused on meaningful, varied, learning experiences. Over-reliance on standards-based instruction makes it difficult for students to connect what they learn in school with life outside of school. School becomes boring, leading many students to disengage. To these students a major purpose of learning—to prepare for college and career—seems becomes unimportant. Their visions of the future weaken.

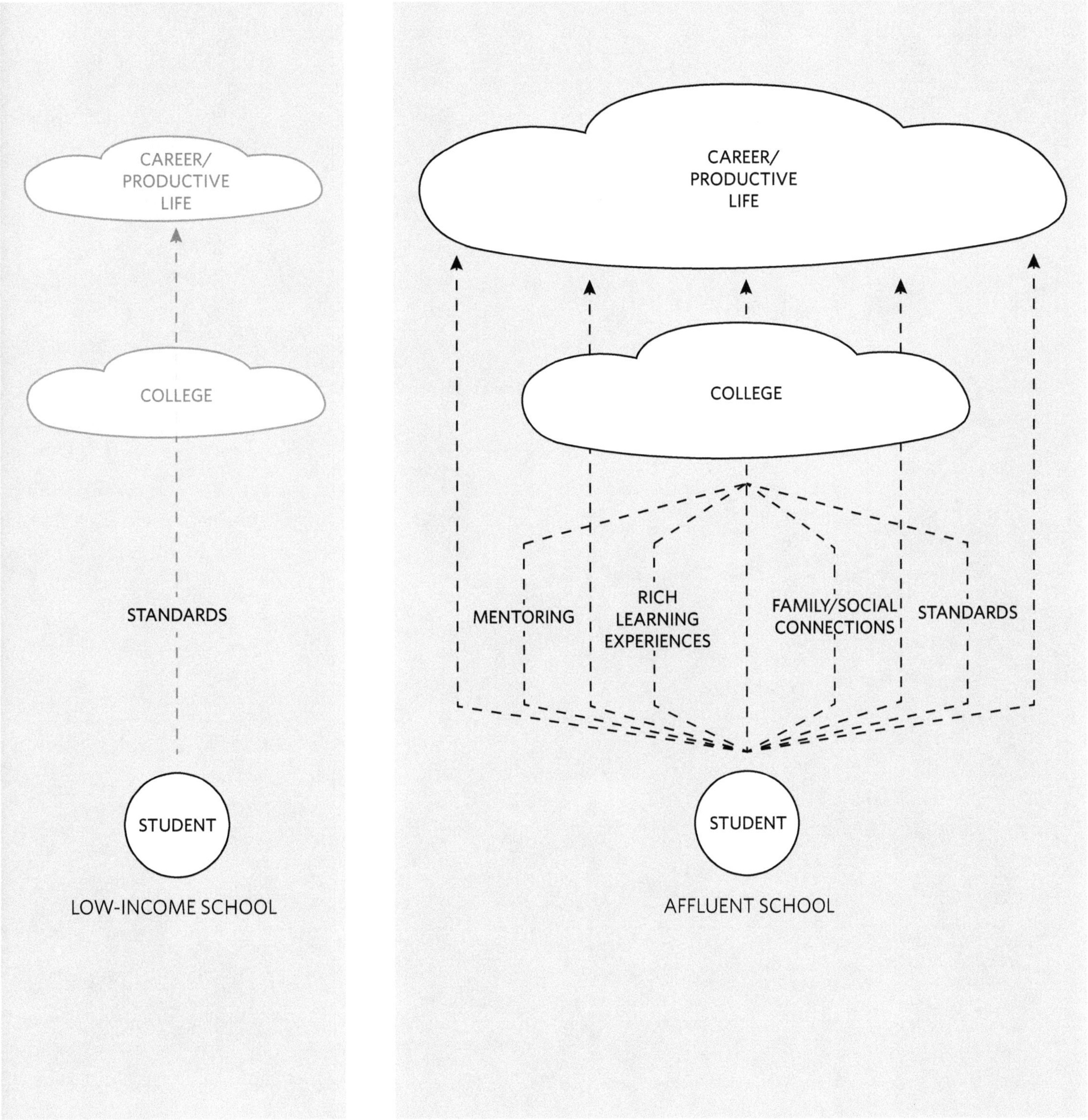

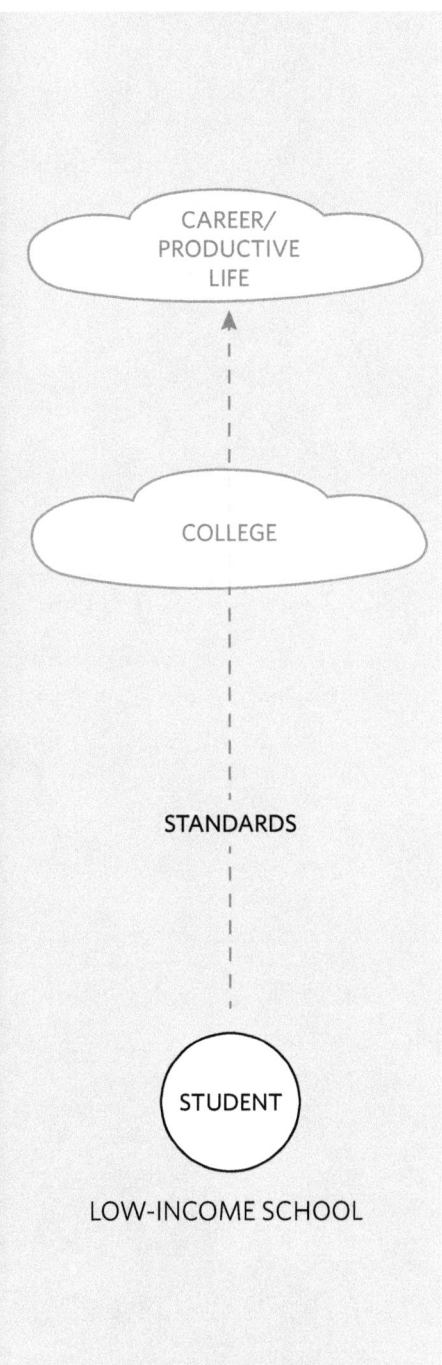

Students at EPIC Academy settle in to work on their online writing portfolios in the computer lab.

Jeff, a computer engineer trained at MIT Media Lab, leads a discussion about sensors in the environment during a meeting of the Northside Prep Thinkering Club.

of what work is really like—help them connect school to their lives and their futures. We call this difference between the experiences of kids in low-income communities and kids in affluent communities the "experience divide." In both low-income and affluent schools, we observed that most kids were motivated to learn skills and concepts when they could see how mastery could help them accomplish something that was meaningful to them. Standards-driven instruction and encouragement from teachers and parents alone are not enough to keep kids engaged.

IMPLICATIONS FOR BETTERAT/SCHOOL
Learning directly from knowledgeable adults outside of school makes learning concrete for kids in ways that conventional textbooks and lectures cannot. Expert-driven learning challenges students to observe how abstract information is applied to concrete problem-solving tasks. It helps them learn how to interact with adults in professional environments, creates valuable feedback loops with those who know the skills and content best, and helps them make important social connections that will become valuable as they advance in education and careers. BetterAt/School makes it easy for teachers to offer these kinds of learning experiences to their students, and remove the logistical barriers that prevent knowledgeable adults in the community from sharing their expertise with those who need it most.

Who actually benefits from standards-driven instruction?

LOW-INCOME STUDENTS
Standards-driven instruction is irrelevant to kids in low-income areas. College and career are far from the norm and many struggle just to remain in school.

MAINSTREAM STUDENTS
Adequately-performing students with strong family support and social norms that reward college matriculation benefit most from standards-driven instruction.

AFFLUENT STUDENTS
High-achieving, highly motivated kids don't need standards-driven instruction. Not only is college a given, but family and social connections are greater factors in their success.

Alicia shares her online portfolio with the research team. Each student at her school creates a digital portfolio of all of their written assignments.

"Our students know the *word* music, but they don't know what goes into composing, producing, or distributing music." —*Dan, principal of an interest-based high school*

EXAMPLE
Alicia is Struggling to Find Her Path
A school with low scores—a girl with high hopes

Alicia is a 10th grader from the south side of Chicago. The school Alicia attends is serious about teaching literacy skills and preparing students for college, and her school's model emphasizes a rigorous academic curriculum. But test scores at her school remain stubbornly low—in 2012 only 16% of students met or exceeded standards on the Prairie State Achievement Exam. Her school's graduation rate is stuck at 61%, and only 60% of those who graduate enroll in college.

In many ways, Alicia is lucky. She has the active support of her family and feels a budding sense of purpose—she is drawn to careers that help people. She has friends and relatives that have been victims of crime, so she has decided to explore a career in law or law enforcement. Her first thought was to become a police officer, but she quickly realized that she wasn't prepared to put her personal safety at risk. Next she considered becoming a detective because that seemed less risky, but then she realized that in order to become a detective, you first have to be a police officer. She then had an opportunity to participate in a mock trial at school where the students played the roles of judge, attorneys, plaintiff, and defendant. This experience captured her imagination and gave her the idea of becoming an attorney.

However, because Alicia and her family don't personally know any police officers, detectives, or attorneys, most of her understanding of law enforcement professionals comes from TV and movies. She hasn't figured out what her next steps might be, beyond working hard. All she knows for sure is that she needs good writing skills.

EXAMPLE

Ahmed Learns by Doing and Thinks by Making

This is what high-performance learning looks like

Ahmed is a junior in a high school on the north side of Chicago. In addition to abundant AP classes, the school Ahmed attends also offers students the opportunity to enroll in special interest colloquia—courses that integrate faculty and student interests into the school curriculum. Ahmed's school is highly selective—it regularly lands on lists of the nation's top public schools—and its students routinely score in the top percentiles on standardized tests.

Ahmed is taking a colloquium in rebuilding vintage motorcycles this semester. He also joined the computer science club, co-moderated by an engineer from MIT Media Lab and his computer science teacher. The goal is to give students an experience with the entire design and engineering process, from deciding what to make all the way through making it and demonstrating how it works—the way it happens in real life. This year, the club built an electronic recycling bin designed to encourage students to recycle paper more responsibly.

Ahmed often wears a t-shirt that says it all: "This is what a computer scientist looks like." He has no trouble envisioning his future. His first-hand experience with the computer science club and the informal conversations he has had with friends of his parents and his friends' parents (who are engineers) have given him a good idea of what computer scientists do. He knows what his next steps are: getting internships at engineering offices, narrowing down his list of good engineering programs, writing essays, submitting applications, visiting colleges, and making his final decision.

Ahmed prepares the Thinkering Club's Smart Recycle Bin project for presentation to prospective students and parents at his school's annual open house. The Smart Recycle Bin encourages kids to recycle by providing a clever animation on a screen above the bin that pictures a tree growing every time a piece of paper is dropped in.

What if Alicia had direct access to an expert—a practicing criminal defense attorney or civil rights attorney—so she could ask her own questions?
What if she had an opportunity to solve a real-life problem with an expert's guidance?

EXPERT CHALLENGES WILL ENABLE STUDENTS TO...
- apply abstract knowledge to concrete problem-solving tasks
- experience workplace etiquette
- experience how work is evaluated in a professional setting
- experience how social and professional networks support college and career paths

CONCEPT
Expert Challenges
Engaging students by engaging the real world

BetterAt/School will make it easy for students to engage with experts through expert challenges such as "Has the Legal System Changed for Minority Teens?" which explores the practice of law, our criminal justice system, and the legacy of civil rights in the US. Each expert challenge will be designed to immerse students in a real-world problem through a set of activities that requires them to gain an understanding of the problem (and its root causes and drivers) and then create innovative solutions. All challenges will be mapped to the Common Core State Standards, instruction will be based on the BetterAt/School instructional framework, and activities will be based on the BetterAt/School activity framework.

❺ LOCAL EXPERT
Students interview either an expert from the civic learning network's expert network or an expert they personally know.

❻ STUDENT WORK
Students complete the tasks outlined in the challenge and upload their work (or sync using BetterAt/apps) directly into their timeline.

[Sync]

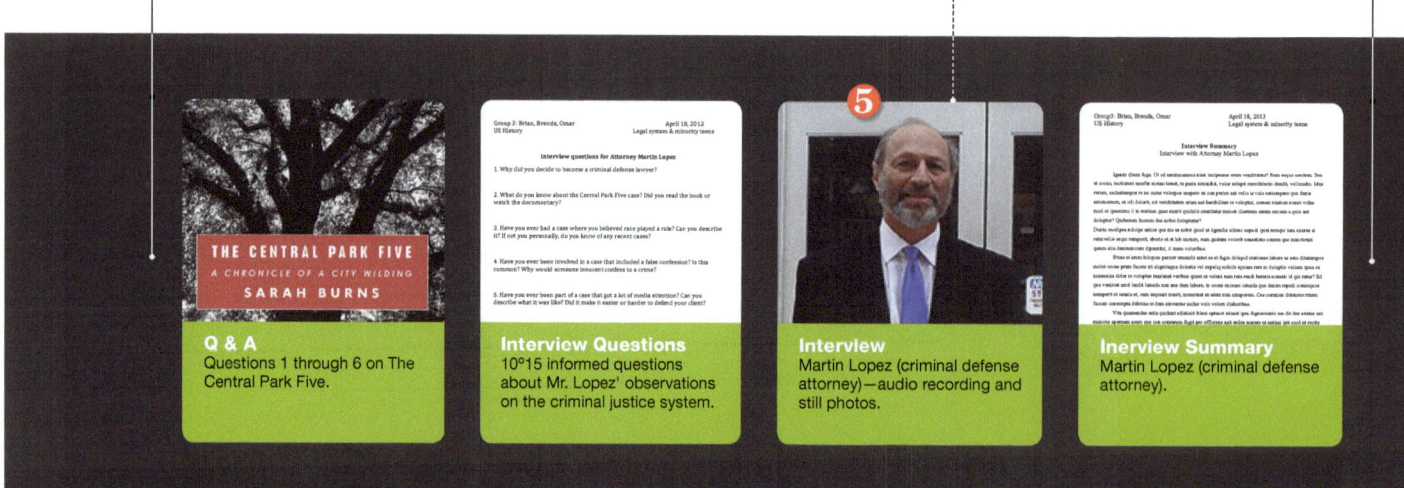

Expert Challenge:
Has the Legal System Changed for Minority Teens?

❶ What will I learn?

In this challenge, you will work in groups to:

1. Describe the *Central Park Five* case using legal terminology and explain how and why five people were found guilty of a crime they did not commit.
2. Describe the societal conditions of New York City in the 1980s/1990s that contributed to the proceedings and outcome of the case.
3. Using edivdence, argue whether or not the legal system can be "blind" to race, color, age, or other factors.
4. Write interview questions that are informed, unbiased, and that will produce high-quality, reliable information.
5. Conduct a formal interview with a legal professional that demonstrates your understanding of the case and of the legal system.

This challenge is aligned with: CCSS.ELA-Literacy.CCRA.R.1; CCSS.ELA-Literacy. CCRA.R.2; CCSS.ELA-Literacy.RH.11-12.3; CCSS.ELA-Literacy. RH.11-12.4; CCSS.ELA-Literacy.RH.11-12.8

❷ How will I learn it?

Choose four questions to answer during and after your reading. Each answer should be about a paragraph long. Each group member should answer separately. Upload to your group's timeline.

1. How does Burns describe New York in the 1980s? What imagery does she use to convey the mood of the city?
2. Imagine you were making a collage of the mood of NYC in the 1980s. Find three to five photos that would convey the mood. Attach the photos into this step.
3. Compare Burns's New York of the late '80s and early '90s to your city today. What similarities are there? What differences?
4. What historical examples of racial violence does Burns give in the book? Why is this important to know within the context of the Central Park case?
5. Burns uses the word "we" (such as that this case shows us "who and what we fear.") Who is "we"? What is the danger of using this type of vocabulary?
6. The "war on terror" has changed the way we think about the legal and ethical issues of interrogation tactics and the consequences of presuming guilt when investigating a case. Does this story tell us anything about the way our society sees criminals?
7. What do you believe are our legal system's greatest problems? Why?

❸ What will I do?

Task 11 (Informational or Explanatory/Definition)

8. Using the background information you have gained through reading and watching excerpts of "Central Park Five" and answering the comprehension questions, write a series of 10 to 15 informed interview questions that explore a legal expert's observations on how the legal system has changed since the late 1980s/early 1990s. Upload to your group's timeline.
9. As a group, conduct an interview with a local expert. Capture your interview with photos, audio recording, video or written notes. Together, write a summary of your interview. Upload to your group's timeline.
10. Together, create a final presentation (e. g., slide presentation or video) that includes a summary of what you learned in your research, your point of view on whether the legal system has changed meaningfully since then, and recommendations for ways the system can be improved.

❹ How will I assess my work?

As a group, use the rubric to evaluate your presentation's first draft. Is there anything you can improve upon? Go back and do it! When your group has completed your final draft, use the rubric again to score yourself. For each category, give yourself a score between 1-4. Share your score in the comment section of this step. Refer to your self-assessment when conferencing with your teacher about your work.

❶ What will I learn?
I will learn how the justice system treats minorities and whether it is changing.

❷ Interview Questions
10°15 informed questions about Mr. Lopez' observations on the criminal justice system.

❸ Interview
Martin Lopez (criminal defense attorney)—audio recording and still photos.

❹ Inerview Summary
Martin Lopez (criminal defense attorney).

The Instructional Framework

BetterAt learning activities (expert challenges and starter plans) follow a four-part structure to ensure that all participants and stakeholders—students, teachers, mentors, and parents—have a shared understanding of an activity's purpose and goals. Like the Literacy Design Collaborative instructional framework on which it is based (see page 32), the BetterAt instructional framework focuses on a specific teaching task and includes skills, a series of tasks to guide instruction, and a scoring guide to assess student performance. Unlike the LDC framework, this model uses student language so that students and teachers have a shared understanding of the process and goals and so that students possess greater ownership of the learning.

❶ What will I learn?

As the first step, this lays the groundwork for the activity and communicates why and how it is relevant to the student. It outlines the objective of the learning activity in terms of what a student should know and be able to do by the end of the activity. This includes knowledge, skills, and processes.

❷ How will I learn it?

In this step, the learner uses resources and processes to gather information. This step most closely correlates with mainstream classroom content delivery, but also emphasizes nontraditional methods of discovery. This may include consuming print and digital media, interacting with experts, teachers, mentors, peers, and/or conducting research.

❸ What will I do?

This step outlines and describes actions that will reinforce the learning and demonstrate understanding of concepts. In this step, students will apply what they learned in step 2 to solve real-world problems and will create products that reveal those learnings.

❹ How will I assess my work?

This step outlines how a student's learning, and the products he or she has created, will be assessed. This step includes a CCSS- aligned rubric written in learner language that is used by both the teacher and the student. The teacher's assessment of the work and the student's self-assessment are always part of the activity. Peer assessment may also be part of the process. The rubric is not only an assessment tool but a conversation starter and is meant to lay the foundation of meaningful teacher feedback and student reflection.

Expert Challenges—How They Work

Expert challenges can be integrated into any type of classroom. In an interest-based classroom, students would be involved in directing the work. In a curriculum-driven classroom, the teacher would take a more active role in managing the project.

Interest-based classroom

Preview Teacher tells students about the project beforehand; kids look at it, read through first step, and decide if they want to do it.

→ **Day 1** Students view author's message either individually or in small groups and decide which final product they will create.

→ **Day 2** Students choose from plan which resources they want to use (e.g., excerpts from book or documentary), and get them from teacher.

Day 3 Students work independently or in small groups to write questions and discuss final product. Students select an expert to interview and set up the appointment.

→ **Day 4** Students conduct the interview(s) individually or in small groups and upload to or sync their work with their BetterAt/School timeline.

→ **Day 5** Students work on their own or in groups to create final product and share on BetterAt/School.

Curriculum-driven classroom

Preview Teacher picks a class to do activity with and may edit the plan if needed. Teacher arranges ahead of time for an expert to come to class to meet with students.

→ **Day 1** Class reads through step 1 ("What will I do?") and watches message from author together.

→ **Day 2** Teacher provides students with resources; students read entire book or excerpts chosen by teacher or watch documentary.

Day 3 Students work in small groups to write questions and decide final product (options are provided in challenge and choice may be guided by teacher).

→ **Day 4** Expert visits the classroom. Interviews are conducted, either with the whole class or in small groups. All student work is either uploaded to or synced with their BetterAt/School timelines.

→ **Day 5** Students work in groups to create final product and share on BetterAt/School.

CONCEPT
Civic Learning Network
Moving from schools as stand-alone institutions to schools as nodes in a network

The civic learning network is a platform that enables a variety of institutions of informal learning (IIL) and other public or private organizations to create content that kids can use to advance their knowledge and abilities in topics of interest to them. IILs come in three main forms: public or private libraries; curatorial organizations, like museums and zoos, that develop coherent points of view; and smaller community organizations, like the Old Town School of Folk Music in Chicago, that help people get better at hobbies and interests. Other potential participants include public and private organizations, such as professional or trade organizations like the American Bar Association or International Brotherhood of Electrical Workers, that help set standards and practices for a particular field and corporations and small businesses with a strong social mission, professional expertise to share, and an interest in serving youth.

The civic learning network will do this by being designed and optimized for an individual kid's interests. The network will create the opportunity to combine the efficiency of formal learning with the effectiveness and enjoyment of informal learning. This will be made possible by leveraging the formal learning features of BetterAt/School with characteristics of the socially based, informal learning that is core to after-school programs and other events currently conducted in IILs. To enable this change, two challenges or opportunities need to be met:

1. Combine the rigor of formal learning with the relevance of informal learning.
2. In curatorial institutions, resolve the conflict between curatorial excellence and public popularity.

The following design principles have informed the development of the civic learning network concept:
- Learning should be interest-driven, social, and experience-based.
- Informal learning should be brought into the formal environment and vice-versa.
- The social conditions for learning in schools should be grounded in real-world, inspiring experiences.
- Museum staff expertise and content should be dispersed into the public realm.
- Institutions should act as nodes on a network, not remote islands of knowledge.

The Civic Learning Network

The civic learning network is designed to enable institutions of informal learning (IILs) to better meet the needs of the communities they serve. BetterAt/School's technology platform and BetterAt/School learning design services will make it easy for member institutions to share expertise and resources with schools and individuals—in ways that are most helpful to users themselves.

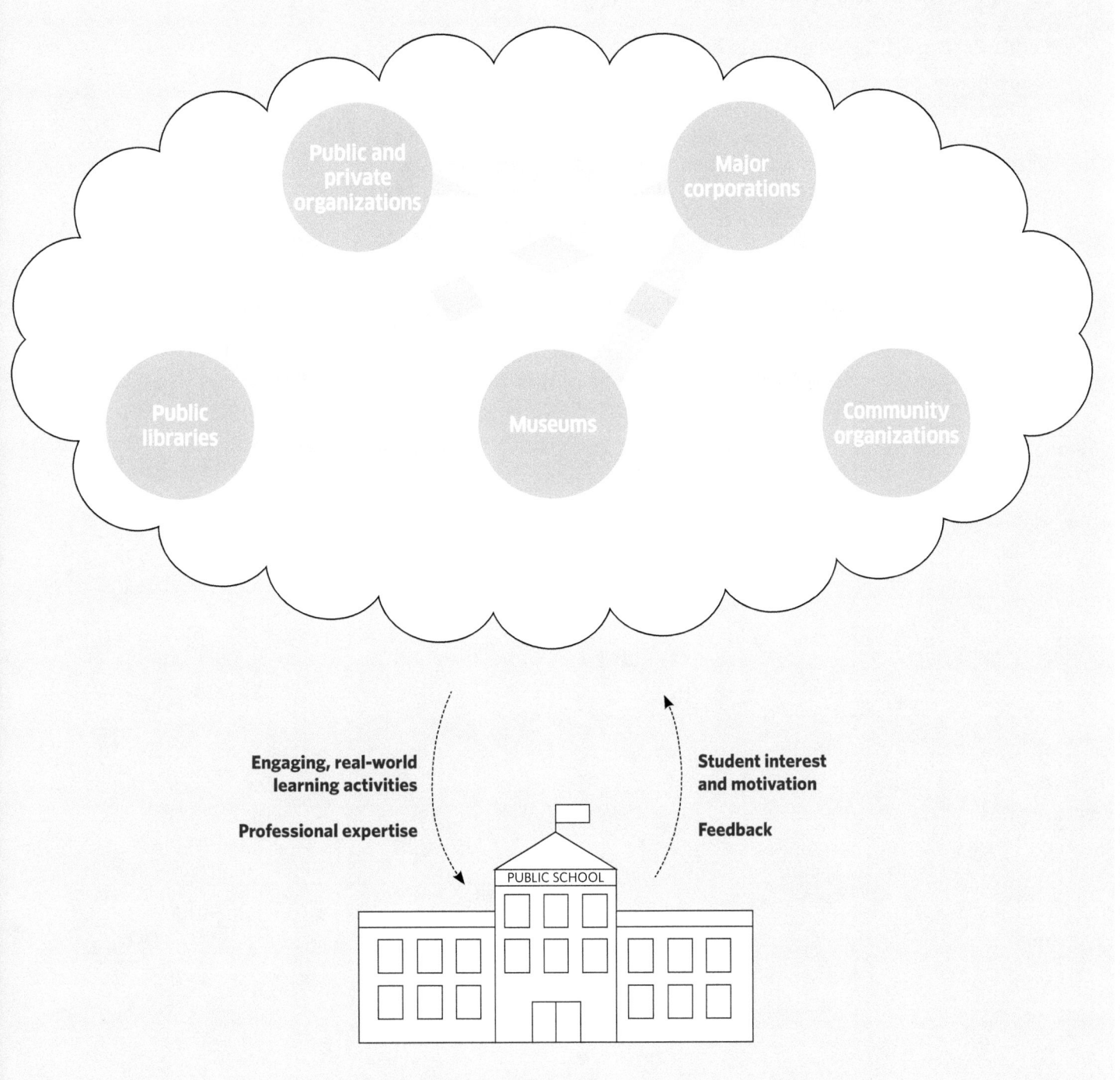

CONCEPT
Expert Network
Connecting students directly to professional expertise

The BetterAt/School *Expert Network* is a clearinghouse within the civic learning network for expert knowledge and mentoring that will provide students with opportunities to learn directly from adults with professional expertise. Experts will be recruited from within the institutions of informal learning, professional and trade organizations, and companies that are part of the civic learning network. Each expert who joins the network will apply for BetterAt/School expert certification.

Experts may choose to participate in the expert network by taking part in a learning design workshop offered by BetterAt/School learning design services and then author an expert challenge. Expert challenge authoring supports a wide range of options for student interaction, from prerecorded messages and instructions for live video conferencing to online feedback in real time and face-to-face encounters with groups or classes in schools or the expert's home institution.

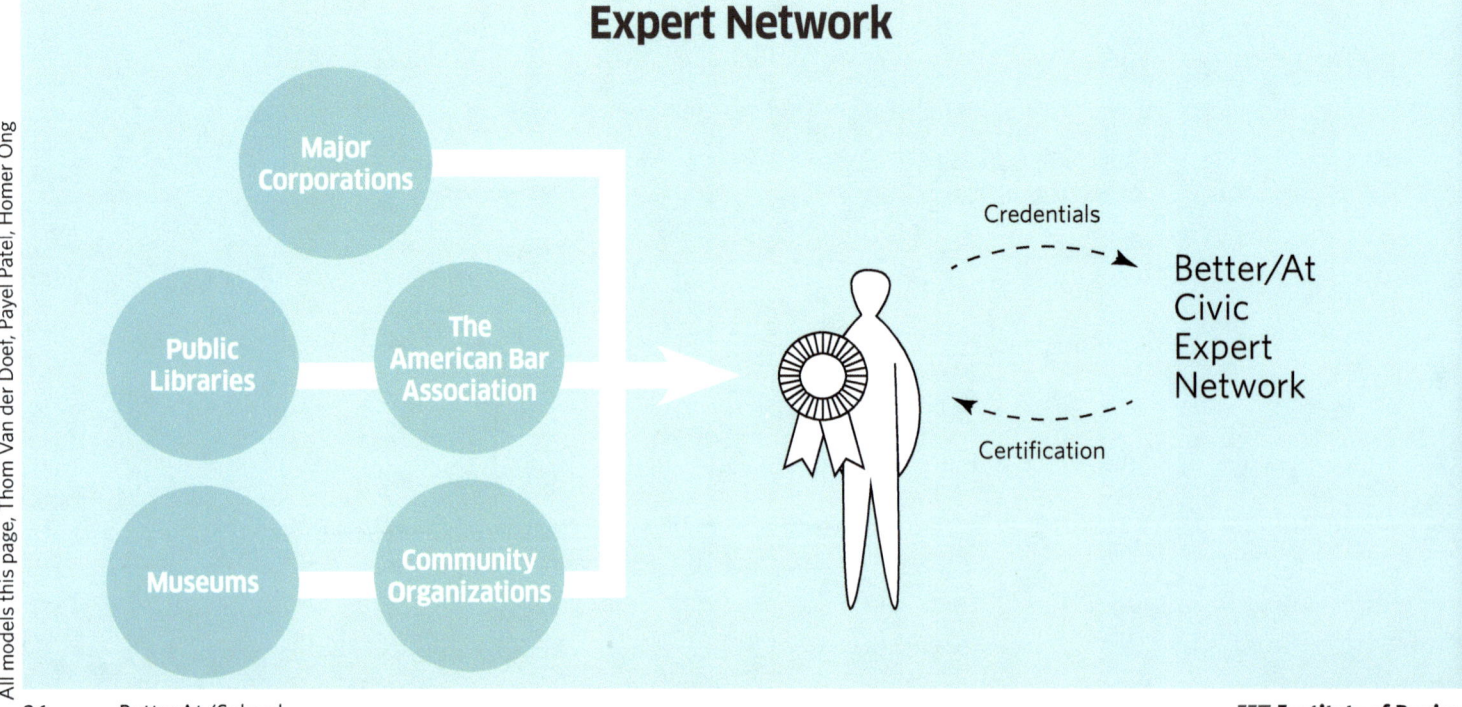

CONCEPT
Learning Design Services
Supporting change, creating content

Organizations need help overcoming barriers to institutional change. For institutions interested in joining the civic learning network, BetterAt/School learning design services will provide design expertise and guidance in implementing the vision of the civic learning network. BetterAt/School learning design services will take a learner-centered approach to helping institutions respond to the needs of the community.

Through a series of workshops, BetterAt/School learning design services will bring together teachers and experts from the civic learning network to create starter plans and expert challenges. Participants in the workshops will be grouped into cross-disciplinary teams with a teacher, an expert, and a designer. Teams will identify a topic or problem of mutual interest, brainstorm ideas for the learning activity, then combine the best ideas or select the best idea for further development. Guided by the BetterAt/School instructional framework and the BetterAt/School activity framework, teams will then flesh out their modules and present them to a panel of student advisors. Next the teams will present their refined modules to their fellow workshop participants, after which further refinements are made (if needed). The modules will then be published for use on BetterAt/School.

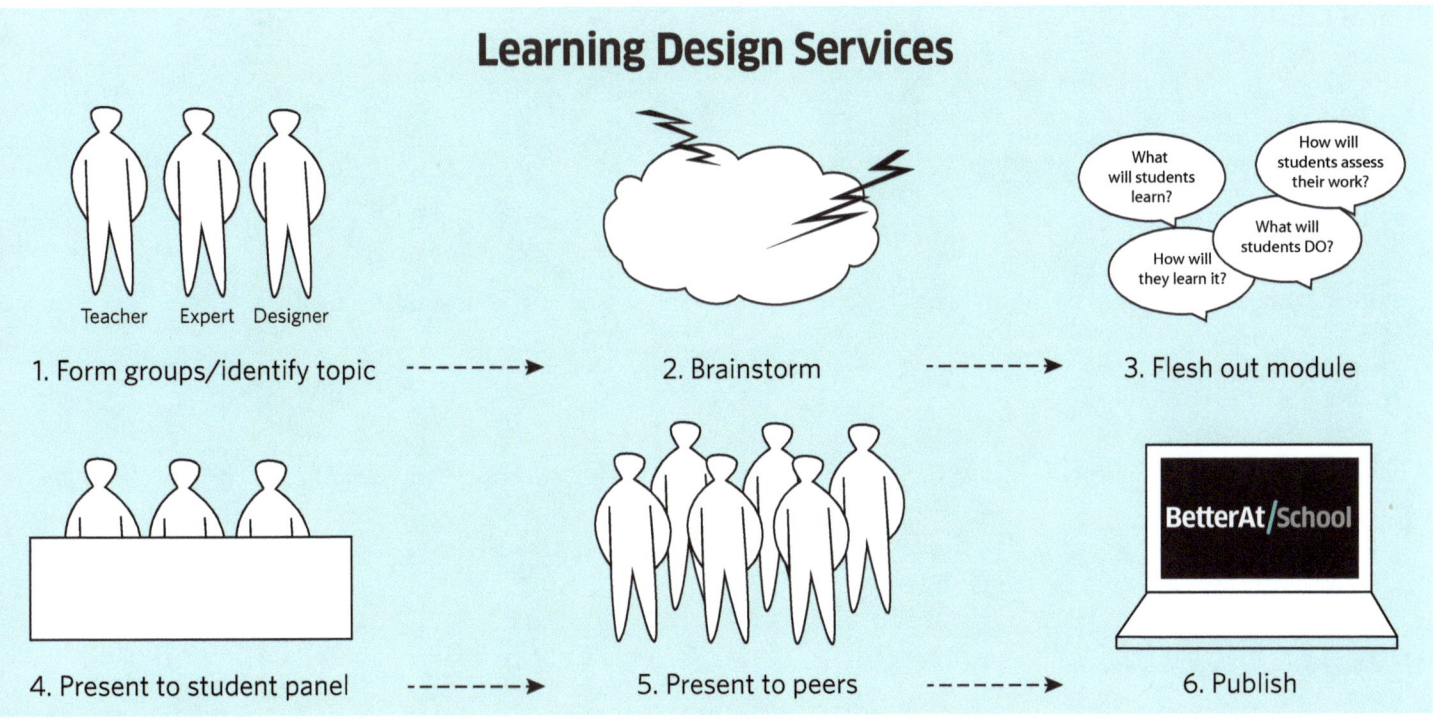

PART 2 TEACHING
For today's teachers, student engagement and academic rigor are competing objectives

The teachers we interviewed in both interest-based schools as well as curriculum-driven schools told us how difficult it is to create lessons that are both engaging and rigorous for every student in their classrooms. We heard how dispiriting it is to feel the pressure of test performance weighing on their shoulders as the wall clock ticks away the minutes in class. We heard how exhilarating it is to see students embrace an activity with gusto—but how a teacher's anxiety often creeps in about whether enough content was covered. And we heard about sleepless nights teachers spend wondering if, despite their best efforts, they are somehow falling short for their students, even though they realize that they can't possibly be experts in everything.

RESEARCH FINDINGS
Teaching Models
Curriculum-driven, interest-based, or project-driven—the landscape of teaching

Our research revealed three dominant teaching models in American public schools. We observed that almost all schools can be defined as either curriculum driven or interest based, but teachers in both reported that it was important to incorporate project-driven methods wherever possible.

1. CURRICULUM-DRIVEN
Curriculum-driven teaching is the mainstream. Predictive in nature, a curriculum-driven teacher plans lessons and delivers content to students and expects students to reach certain milestones at predictable points in the school year (for example, at the end of a unit, at mid-term, at the end of the term, at the end of the year). Tests, standards-aligned textbooks, and syllabi are the tools that support curriculum-driven learning. Assessment is straightforward—a teacher or testing company creates an instrument that assesses student mastery of content or skills at a single point in time. The syllabus indicates the content to be delivered; the test confirms how much of the content was mastered by the student.

2. INTEREST-BASED
At the other end of the spectrum and at the edges of the mainstream is interest-based teaching. Responsive in nature, an interest-based teacher's job is not to predict learning outcomes but to set the conditions for learning. Students drive the curriculum, and pacing is determined not by the classroom clock or the school calendar but by the student's needs. Assessment requires many more points of contact between teacher and student, and in addition to mastery of content, the student must also demonstrate mastery of his or her own learning process and an ability to apply that learning to real life.

3. PROJECT-DRIVEN
Project-driven teaching can exist within either environment. In an interest-based classroom, the project will be an individual project. Teachers who assign projects accept the additional labor required to manage and assess student work. Assessment is centered on the reports, models, and presentations that students produce as documentation of their work. Projects are usually bounded by a fixed time schedule, but unlike regular lessons, it is less certain that all the content to be covered will be covered by the student. For this reason, project-driven teaching works best in schools where students are highly motivated and willing to take initiative.

IMPLICATIONS FOR BETTERAT/SCHOOL
While our research suggests strongly that interest-based methods are most successful in helping low-income students engage in school, the vast majority of low-income kids in the United States attend curriculum-driven schools. For this reason, it will be important for BetterAt/School to develop solutions that integrate interest-based methods into learning activities that curriculum-driven teachers can readily adopt.

Teaching Models Defined

The BetterAt/School research team looked closely at the defining characteristics of interest-based teaching, curriculum-driven teaching, and project-driven teaching in order to identify the risks and potential rewards of each model.

Responsive teaching protocols are designed to achieve the goals set by the student with the active help of the teacher.

Predictive teaching protocols are designed to achieve the goals set by the teacher.

	INTEREST-BASED	CURRICULUM-DRIVEN	PROJECT-DRIVEN
Protocol	Responsive	Predictive	Both predictive and responsive
Control	Student led	Teacher led	Collaborative
Structure	One-to-one	One-to-all	One-to-groups in curriculum-driven classroom; one-to-one in interest-based classroom
Assessment	Optimized for process assessment	Optimized for standardized testing	Optimized for process assessment
Key Beneficiaries	Unmotivated, under-achieving outliers	Adequately motivated, average mainstream kids	Highly motivated, high-achieving outliers

Interest-based methods help unmotivated kids develop personal interests into career goals and help them connect learning in school with success in life. Mentors, internship supervisors, and other interested adults help the teacher provide meaningful guidance to students.

Schools whose students generally meet or exceed proficiency on standardized tests and enroll in selective colleges have healthy graduation rates and see no value in risking their academic standing by experimenting with interest-based or project-based methods.

Project-driven teaching requires more effort on the part of teachers and compromises the predictability of the teacher's lesson plan. Project-driven teaching is most successful in schools with students who are highly motivated and whose parents have high expectations.

IIT Institute of Design

"I want to be an entrepreneur because you're your own boss. I want to have an entertainment business. I want to be in charge of all of it. I want it to be not just one specific entertainment. I want it to be different entertainment and I'm the boss of it all."—Monique, student

How Kids Discover Interests
Moving from confusion, serendipity, and discovery to realization

One of the most difficult things about interest-driven learning is where to begin. Many teens have great difficulty identifying what their interests are. Even more difficult for them is identifying interests that can lead to college and career.

THEY DON'T KNOW EXACTLY WHAT THEY'RE INTERESTED IN
In almost every school or youth organization we visited, we noticed that many students struggle to identify their interests. Teachers and counselors try various methods to help students discover and pursue interests. Internships are one way students gain a deeper understanding of their interests and find opportunities to reflect on direct experience and re-assess their interest.

THEY DON'T KNOW HOW TO CATEGORIZE THEIR INTERESTS
Jon, dean of discipline at Gary Comer Prep, likes to talk to students about film. He told us about how a student he recently spoke with couldn't tell him what genre of movies he likes, only that he likes movies. It surprised Jon that the student lacked the language to describe genre.

"Folk categorization," or "vernacular naming," is a solution that Pandora, Netflix, and other recommendation engines have long recognized. Pandora organizes songs not by genre but by qualities like beat or tone of voice. Netflix has replaced labels for action or comedy with more specific descriptions such as "high budget with strong female lead" or "cynical comedy from the 80s." It's possible such folk taxonomies also exist for academic subjects, where students might be interested in events like the Triangle Shirt Factory Fire or other stories from manufacturing, having never heard of larger themes like the Industrial Revolution.

IMPLICATIONS FOR BETTERAT/SCHOOL
The research we conducted in high schools demonstrates that interest is not a binary, static emotion. It is a process that begins with not knowing one's own interests, continues through serendipitous discovery, and culminates in the student's self-identification as interested in a recognizable subject or theme. BetterAt/School will help students distinguish between interests that are more likely versus less likely to lead to career paths as well as learn to assemble learning plans based on their career-oriented interests, supported by rigorous academic exploration.

"An interest is an inclination to notice something, to pay continuing attention to it, and to try and enter into some active relationship with it which seems appropriate to its interesting features."[6]

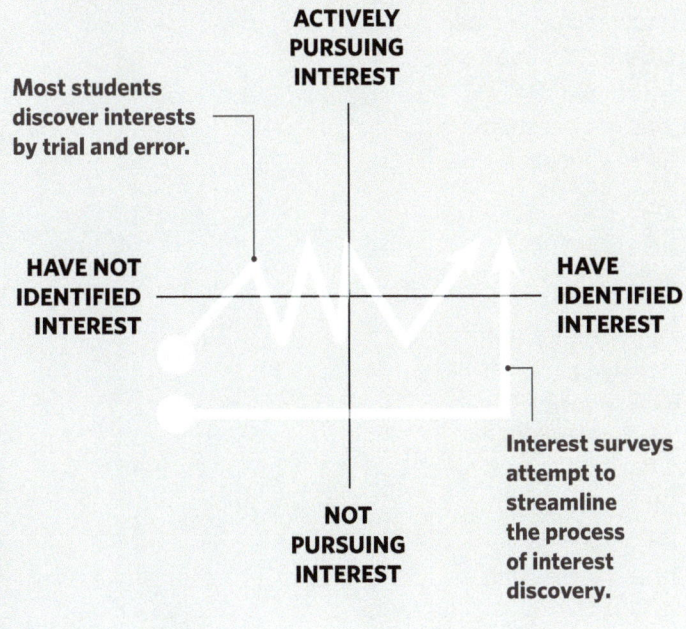

Monique and her mother emigrated from Liberia to Providence, Rhode Island. Here Monique shares her interests in the music business and African cuisine with the BetterAt/School research team.

The Path to Productive Pursuit

Teachers rely on their knowledge and social and professional networks to find resources, mentors, and internships for their students. Students develop their own networks, with different mentors and advisors providing input. It quickly becomes difficult for teachers to monitor these networks and to track student progress.

ACTIVELY PURSUING INTEREST

Most students discover interests by trial and error.

HAVE NOT IDENTIFIED INTEREST — **HAVE IDENTIFIED INTEREST**

Interest surveys attempt to streamline the process of interest discovery.

NOT PURSUING INTEREST

Identifying Interests

Conversations with Bronx Guild teachers and administrators provided a list of ways they identify students' interests and help students identify their own interests.

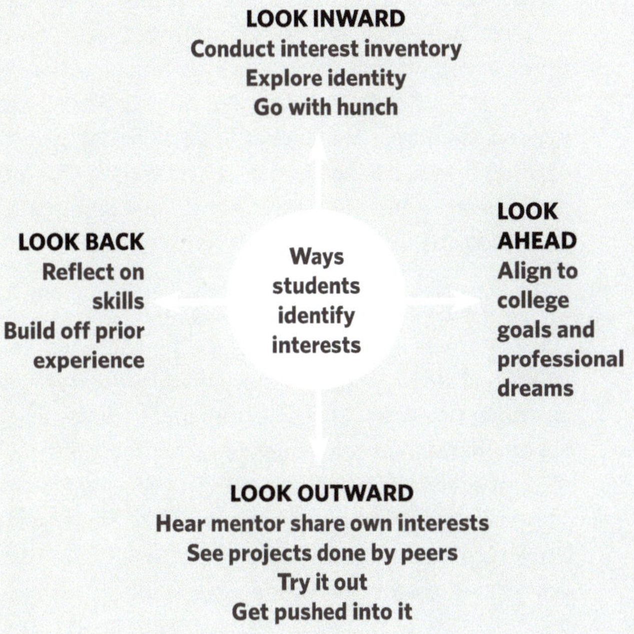

LOOK INWARD
Conduct interest inventory
Explore identity
Go with hunch

LOOK BACK
Reflect on skills
Build off prior experience

Ways students identify interests

LOOK AHEAD
Align to college goals and professional dreams

LOOK OUTWARD
Hear mentor share own interests
See projects done by peers
Try it out
Get pushed into it

IIT Institute of Design

All models this page, Ksenia Pachicov

"We are always telling kids to do what they love and the money will come, but we aren't always backing up that message... [We say,] 'Read a book. Where's the math in this?' Of course that is really important, but that's not what [they're] excited about right now."—*Andrew, administrator*

Interest-Based Learning in Formal Learning Contexts

From delivering content to setting the conditions for learning

The nature of formal learning requires that teachers and students make trade-offs between competing values and goals: activities that take more time versus those that take less, activities that are exploratory in nature versus those that are focused and purposeful, learning much about a few subjects versus learning a little about many subjects. The inclusion of student-centered learning methods in a teacher's practice requires teachers to shift from a predictive model of teaching to a responsive model. Instead of spending time delivering content and creating assessments, an interest-based teacher works hard to set optimal conditions for learning.

NOT ALL INTEREST-BASED ACTIVITIES ARE EQUAL

Interest-driven learning is not always goal-oriented learning. Sometimes students have to decide between doing what is interesting and doing what is relevant to their goal. Without some structure (frameworks, standards, schedules) and the active involvement of interested adults, students may fall into the trap of following their interest without formulating productive goals and plans for achieving them.

TEACHERS' INTERESTS AND EXPERTISE MATTER, TOO

Teachers talked about three kinds of student interests—academic, career, and after school—and they acknowledged that they devote more attention and resources to students' academic and career interests than to students' after-school interests. When asked what students are interested in after school, several teachers named pop music and skateboarding, but quickly dismissed those activities as irrelevant to the classroom. One teacher felt that bringing up these activities was divisive. Another interest-based teacher admitted that he often struggles when a student declares an interest that he doesn't share and many spoke of how difficult it is to guide a student effectively when lacking expertise in that interest.

IMPLICATIONS FOR BETTERAT/SCHOOL

Since interests differ depending on the student, interest-driven learning requires individualized instruction—something mainstream schools are not set up to do. In an interest-based school, mentors and parents take on some teaching responsibility, but an unintended consequence is that teachers—who are still responsible for student academic achievement—now struggle to keep track of each student's resources, activities, and progress. BetterAt/School will make it easier for teachers to oversee student learning as responsibility for instruction and guidance is distributed to other knowledgeable adults.

Beware of Tantalizing Options

Students often fail to discriminate effectively between options in deciding on a path of action.

You are a 15-year-old and your goal for the summer is to become a lifeguard. Which activity do you choose?

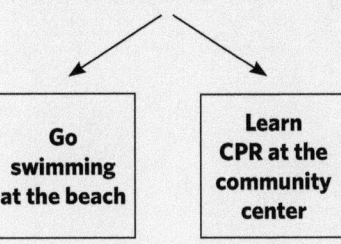

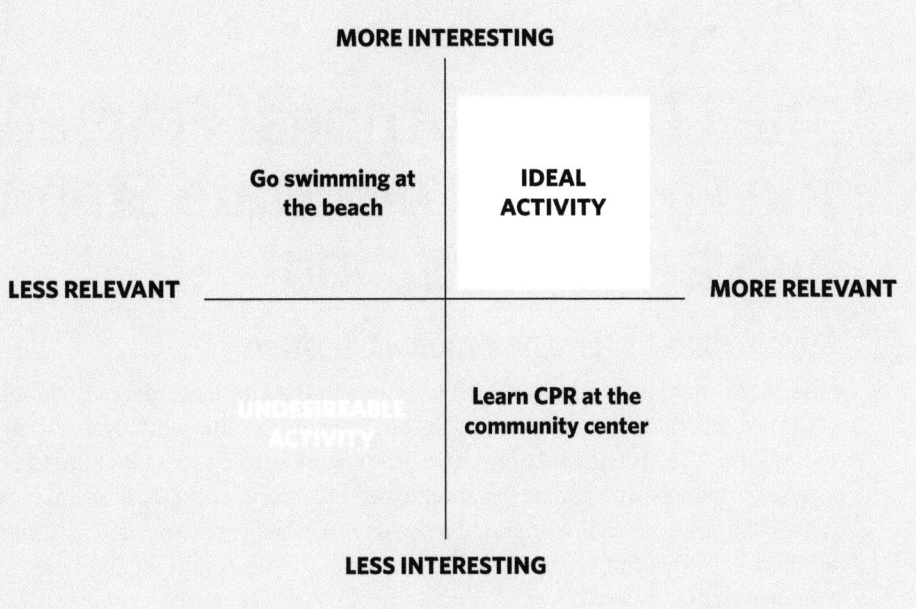

Some Interests Are More Valuable Than Others

Teachers talk about three kinds of student interests: academic, career, and after school. They devote more attention and resources to students' academic and career interests than to their after-school interests.

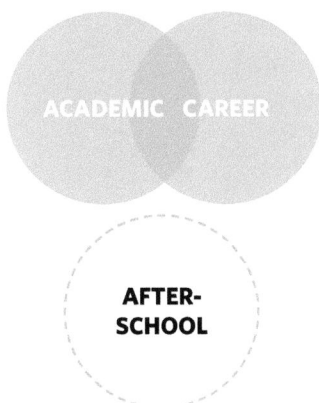

Distributed Instruction

When responsibility for guiding students is shared among appropriate parties, learning can accelerate quickly, but keeping track of student progress becomes more difficult for teachers.

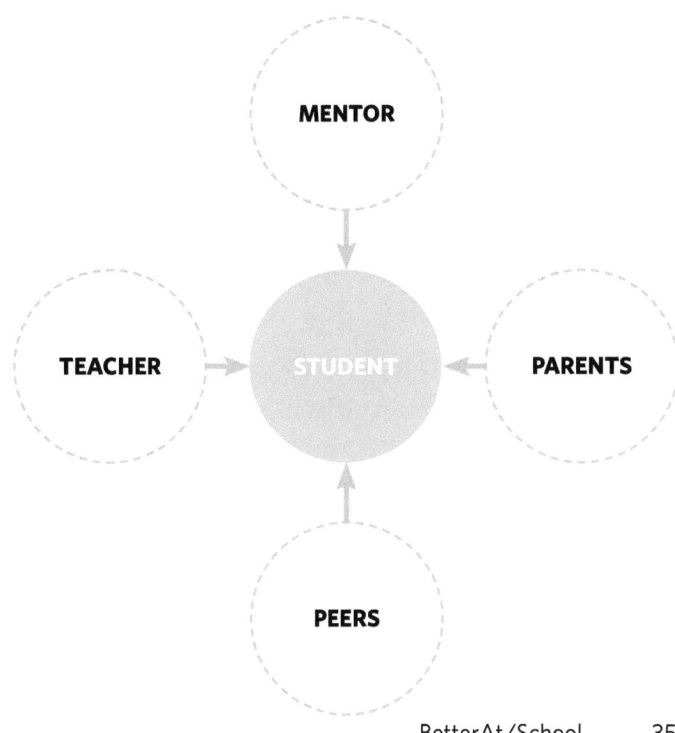

IIT **Institute of Design**

The LDC Instructional Framework, the Common Core State Standards, and BetterAt/School

Building blocks for a new modular system

One of the most important similarities between the Literacy Design Collaborative (LDC) instructional framework and BetterAt/School is that both systems stress modularity. The stated goal of the LDC framework is to enable teachers to create learning modules that can be grouped together to form courses. In a similar way, BetterAt starter plans are intended to be useful initially as short, standalone assignments. In addition, each starter plan can also be combined in myriad ways into projects.

The Common Core Humanities Standards describe baseline proficiencies in the humanities subjects (English language arts, history/social studies, science, and technical subjects). The standards rarely specify content (e.g., Shakespeare's *As You Like It*) and welcome alternative teaching methods. This flexibility of the standards with regard to content and teaching methods aligns with BetterAt/School's focus on student-centered learning. Note that the Common Core Math Standards were not included in this phase of research.

IMPLICATIONS FOR BETTERAT/SCHOOL
While BetterAt/School was not designed to become a channel for disseminating the LDC instructional framework or Common Core State Standards into schools, the research team values both as useful components of a larger solution to the problem of low student engagement. In particular, the LDC instructional framework provided a useful starting point for the development of BetterAt/School's instructional framework. In a similar way, the Common Core State Standards provides a strong starting point for organizing the academic learning component of BetterAt/School's learning activities.

Looking ahead, it will be important to develop additional prototypes in order to refine the BetterAt/School instructional framework and explore additional ways to ensure high-quality, academically rigorous, and logistically feasible plans while at the same time giving teachers and students maximum flexibility to tailor plans to their individual needs. It is also important to explore ways to leverage the learning opportunities embedded in the civic learning network, expert challenges, and expert network within plans in order to maximize the opportunities for students to connect what they are learning in school with real problems in their communities.

The Literacy Design Collaborative (LDC)

The Literacy Design Collaborative (LDC) is a group of classroom teachers, school and district administrators, state departments, state organizations, and education service providers who in 2009 came together and began developing an instructional framework for the Common Core State Standards. The LDC is funded by the Bill & Melinda Gates Foundation.

THE GOAL OF THE LDC
The group's primary goal is to help teachers teach students to meet the common core literacy standards while at the same time meeting local content requirements at a high level of performance. The LDC seeks to do this by creating frameworks and tools to support teachers in implementing the standards.

THE LDC POINT OF VIEW
- Common Core State Standards—The common core standards are a blueprint. They provide a consistent and clear description of what students are expected to learn in order to prepare themselves for success in college and career.
- Student achievement—English language arts instruction in literacy has not been sufficient in advancing literacy among America's young people. Literacy instruction must be the primary focus of learning in school and should be the responsibility of all content areas.
- Opportunity—Standards will be nationwide, so it will be possible to scale practices that work well. Also, since the standards are not content-specific, teachers will be able to use their own judgement and preferences to select content to achieve the literacy standards.

The LDC Framework

The Literacy Design Collaborative describes the framework as a "chassis," a common platform upon which lessons can be constructed. There are three "lenses" in the system— tasks, modules, and courses.

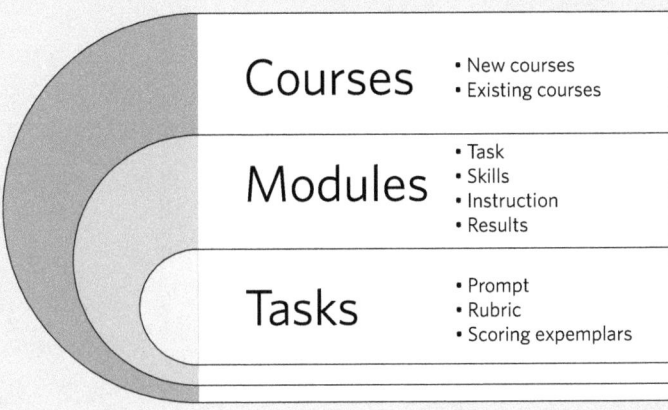

COURSES are made up of modules. Modules can be used as building blocks to create new courses or as options inserted into existing courses.

MODULES provide an instructional plan for teaching the task. It organizes instruction around mini-tasks.

TASKS are reading and writing assignments which challenge students to learn about and discuss an important issue in an academic subject area.

Delia discusses her teaching process at the BetterAt/School Design for Learning Workshop.

EXAMPLE
Delia Feels the Pressures of Standardized Testing

For teachers like Delia, backward planning is just backward

Delia is a teacher at Bronx Guild High School, a small interest-based public school in New York City. While the school's model is unique, Bronx Guild is still subject to the same accountability measures as conventional schools in her state. Delia feels the pressure to make sure all of the experiences she provides her students through internships and interest-based projects align with state and Common Core standards and that her efforts help raise student test performance. She struggles with incorporating standards into the learning activities her students enjoy.

One strategy she uses—backward planning—features a framework that requires teachers to have all of their planning done before starting a new unit. Delia admits that in her six and a half years as a teacher, she has never actually completed the creation of a unit plan before she begins to teach it to her students. Teaching to meet standards requires a predictive planning model so that teachers and administrators can be sure all of the required information will be covered within the course of the semester. However, great interest-based teachers like Delia excel at responsive teaching, using resources and ideas opportunistically to reflect newly discovered resources or to meet the developing needs of their students.

For Delia and her colleagues, planning is not something that happens only before a unit begins but is a constant and sometimes chaotic process of obtaining materials, fleshing out opportunities, and revising plans—all while keeping an eye on the standards and the exams that test them.

What if Delia could easily find plans that were already mapped to the Common Core State Standards and that could be quickly modified to suit different students' needs without losing their rigor?

STARTER PLANS WILL ENABLE TEACHERS TO...
- connect a variety of academic goals to student interests
- help students to maintain focus on purposeful activities related to student interests,
- respond quickly to changing student needs

CONCEPT
Starter Plans
Mixing and remixing great learning ideas—without losing rigor

BetterAt/School will make it easy for teachers to find, mix and remix great learning activities for students with ready-made starter plans that are aligned with the Common Core State Standards. Called starter plans because they form the foundation of a learning activity, these plans are modular and customizable. Like expert challenges, each BetterAt/school starter plan will be built on the BetterAt/School activity framework. The framework will operate as a guide, helping teachers make thoughtful substitutions and changes without compromising the plan's rigor. An interest-based or project-driven teacher might combine several plans into a larger project for a student. Or, a curriculum-driven teacher might augment a lesson with one or two short-duration starter plans to boost student engagement.

❶ BROWSE PLANS
We watched teachers (and students) using BetterAt/School for the first time and saw that the very first thing everyone tried to do was to browse existing content in order to get ideas about what they wanted to do.

❷ STANDARDS PREVIEW
Mousing over a plan activates a window that previews the Common Core State Standards that are aligned with the plan.

❸ EDIT PLAN CONTENTS
will make it easy for teachers to change the order of steps in a plan, or to delete steps.

❹ ADD TO PLAN
will make it easy for teachers to add steps to a plan by choosing the type of media or activity they desire. READ adds a book or other written material; WATCH adds a video; VISIT adds a place; ATTEND adds an event; LINK adds a hyperlink; LISTEN adds a podcast or other audio recording.

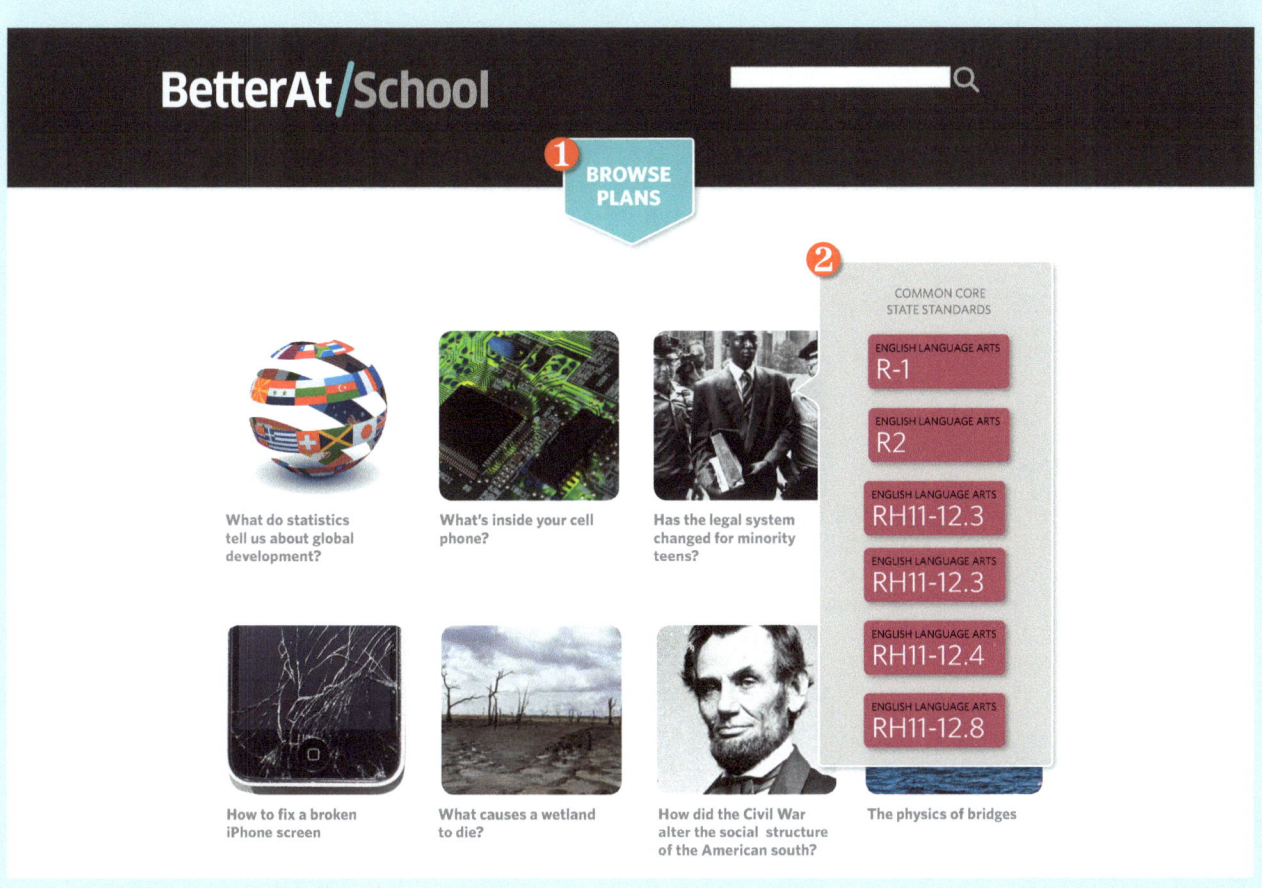
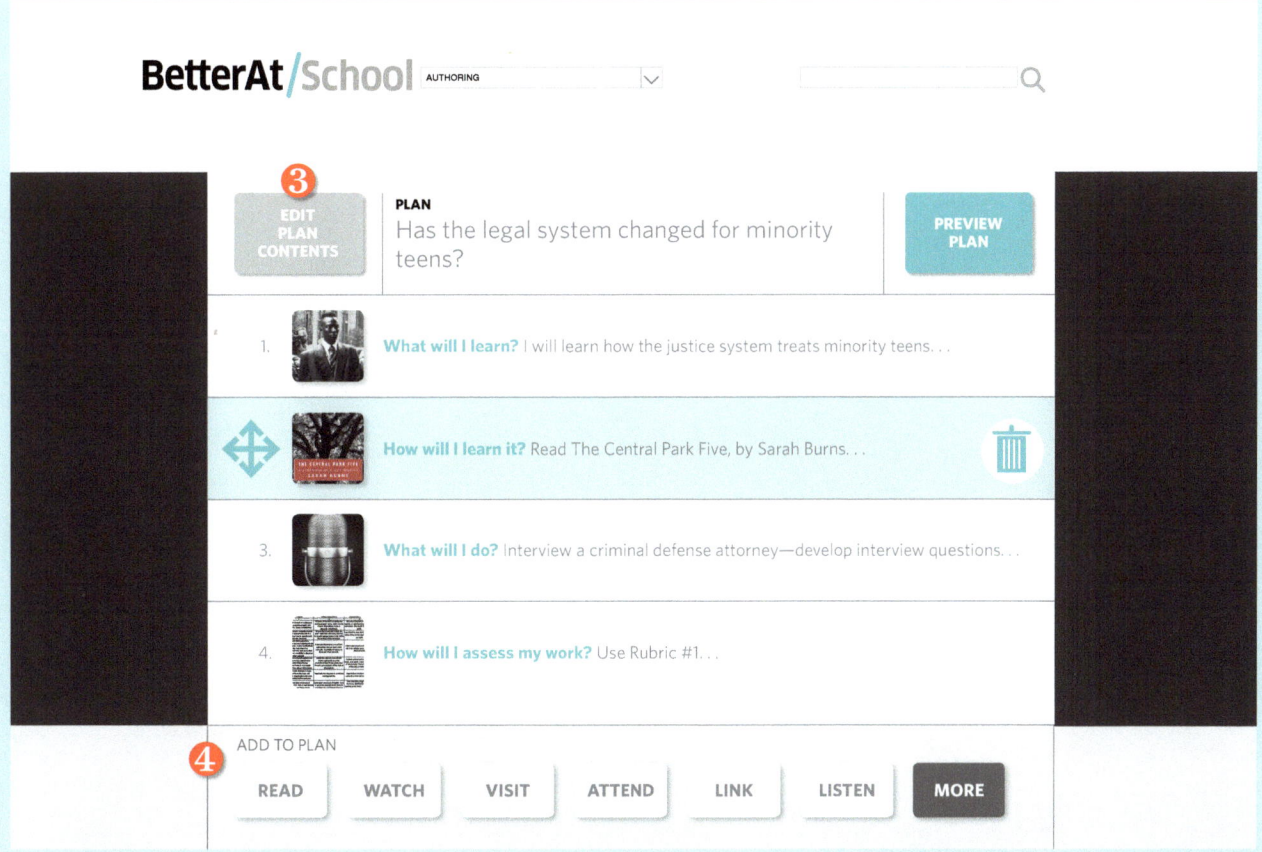

Starter Plans—How They Work in Different Classrooms

Starter plans can be integrated into any type of classroom. In an interest-based classroom, a starter plan would most often be executed by an individual student, and the student would enjoy significant latitude in tailoring the plans to his or her own needs. In a curriculum-driven classroom, a teacher would likely assign the plan to small groups, and the teacher would initiate modifications necessary to meet students' needs.

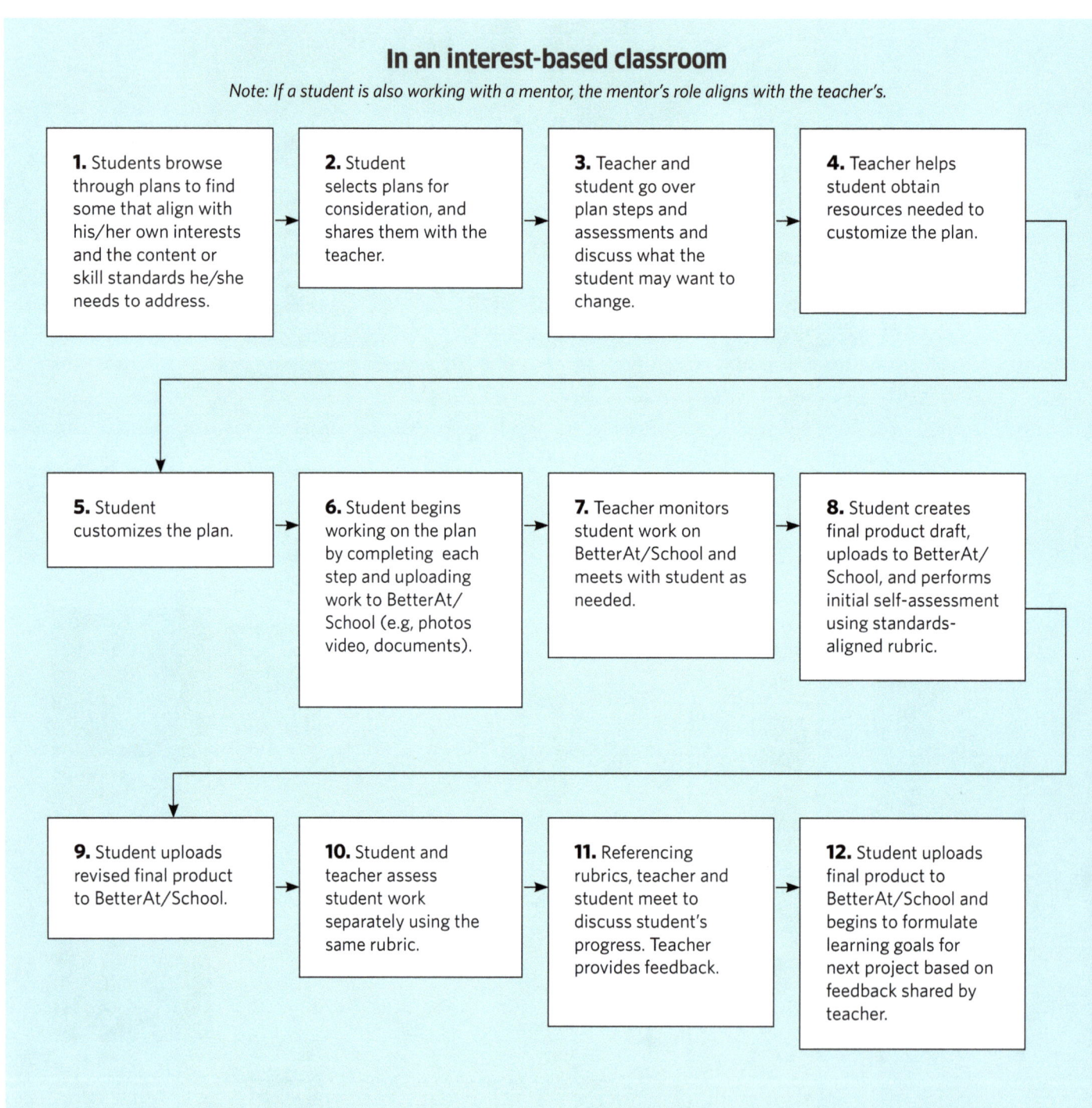

In an interest-based classroom
Note: If a student is also working with a mentor, the mentor's role aligns with the teacher's.

1. Students browse through plans to find some that align with his/her own interests and the content or skill standards he/she needs to address.

2. Student selects plans for consideration, and shares them with the teacher.

3. Teacher and student go over plan steps and assessments and discuss what the student may want to change.

4. Teacher helps student obtain resources needed to customize the plan.

5. Student customizes the plan.

6. Student begins working on the plan by completing each step and uploading work to BetterAt/School (e.g, photos video, documents).

7. Teacher monitors student work on BetterAt/School and meets with student as needed.

8. Student creates final product draft, uploads to BetterAt/School, and performs initial self-assessment using standards-aligned rubric.

9. Student uploads revised final product to BetterAt/School.

10. Student and teacher assess student work separately using the same rubric.

11. Referencing rubrics, teacher and student meet to discuss student's progress. Teacher provides feedback.

12. Student uploads final product to BetterAt/School and begins to formulate learning goals for next project based on feedback shared by teacher.

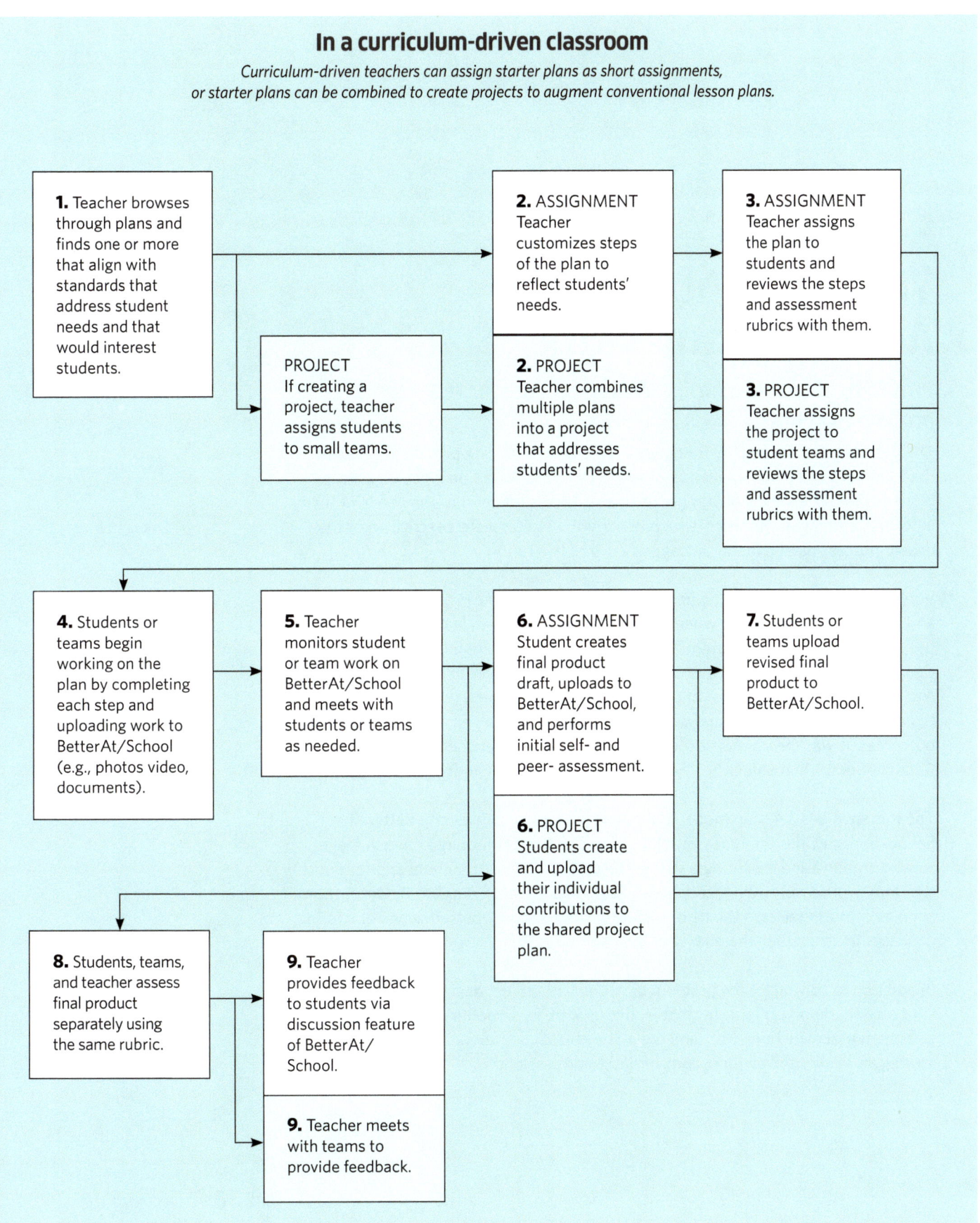

CONCEPT

The BetterAt/School Activity Framework

Providing students a design-driven process for real-world problem solving

The BetterAt/School activity framework is a problem-solving process that forms the foundation of expert challenges and starter plans. Based on a design process pioneered at IIT Institute of Design, the framework is adapted to the needs of teens in formal learning environments such as schools. (A complete description of the design process can be found on pages 52–69 of this report.)

Very early on in our research it became clear that one of the problems students and teachers struggled with when attempting project-driven learning was that they lacked a reliable, consistent framework for planning, organizing, and executing rigorous projects. The team was further struck by the similarity of the students' and teachers' dilemma to that of designers initiating research projects and trying to carefully define research and development plans that will ensure successful outcomes. It was clear that the tools commonly used by teachers and students (Google Docs, Microsoft Office, Facebook, e-mail) were of limited help for this task.

The framework is a 4-step model that builds learning activities into BetterAt/School and specifies the types of activities and outcomes required of each stage toward creating and executing a successful project. BetterAt/School apps support the framework by providing students tools to help them accomplish different tasks such as capturing data in the field, sorting data to discover patterns, and clustering concepts to strengthen the quality of their solutions.

In addition to solving for the problem of haphazard project design, the framework supports an important long-term objective as well: as students gain proficiency in using the *Activity Framework* and tools, they build competencies in innovation strategy already used by thousands of design professionals.

The BetterAt/School Activity Framework

The BetterAt/School activity framework is designed to help students and teachers replicate great learning experiences. It works seamlessly with the BetterAt/School instructional framework and provides guidance for solving the logistical and practical challenges of creating rigorous and interesting student projects.

❶ Research the problem and the people affected by it.

The first step in any project is to conduct primary (observational) and secondary (bibliographic) research in order to find out what is already known about the problem. The outcome (deliverable) of this step is a summary that includes an initial problem statement and a point of view.

❷ Tell us how to think about the problem.

The learner reviews the data he or she has collected and looks for meaningful patterns in activities, behavior, or other phenomena. In addition, the learner is challenged to identify tensions and paradoxes that help explain what is happening in the context in which the problem is occurring and discover the underlying root causes of the problem. The outcome of this step is a revised problem statement (or reframe), a more nuanced point of view, and a set of design principles to guide the development of solutions to the problem.

❸ Brainstorm ideas and solutions.

Students brainstorm ways to solve the problem by first identifying individual concepts that solve parts (but perhaps not all) of the problem. Then they work to combine the concepts into systematic solutions with one or more user types in mind. The outcome of this step is a concise "elevator pitch" and set of sketches, diagrams, or storyboards that describe the solution(s) in detail.

❹ Make your case to others.

Students create a narrative that communicates their solution and their process for others to evaluate. The outcome of this step is usually a report, a presentation, a blog, or a video that frames the work that was done and highlights key learning moments in the process.

PART 3 ASSESSING

Assessing students' knowledge of facts is easy. Assessing students' ability to apply what they've learned is much harder.

It's no secret that critical thinking and problem solving skills are much more valuable in today's economy than the simple knowledge of facts. In order to prepare students for successful careers, schools must teach them how to follow a process—how to create, apply, follow, revise, evaluate, and reflect—and how to use newly acquired knowledge to accomplish their goals. Standardized assessments, by and large, test mastery of knowledge. But measuring students' mastery of the skills and capabilities they need to succeed in today's economy is very difficult—to administer to scale. Unfortunately, these difficulties often prevent curriculum-driven teachers from adopting methods that engage students more actively in learning.

> "Often times in projects, the content is heavily pushed as the most important thing, and the process falls to the wayside. I think students often miss opportunities when reflecting. They're focusing on the content piece—they think about what they could have included rather than thinking, 'How did I go about this?'"—*Paul, high school teacher*

RESEARCH FINDINGS
Process Assessment
Making the learning process seamless from end to end

Assessment—meant to inform teaching, promote learning, and communicate what is worth knowing and being able to do[7]—has become a high stakes experience for most students and their teachers, yet education experts agree that while testing is one way, it is often not the most accurate way to measure a student's knowledge and abilities. Standardized assessments are useful for revealing what a student knows, but they do little to reveal how a student works through a problem.

Process assessment provides information about a student's learning strategies and thinking processes. It reveals what a student can *do* with the knowledge he or she has gained. Many of the teachers we interviewed stressed to us the importance of process assessment but also expressed frustration at not being able to "do it right." Process assessment *is* difficult—it is time-consuming and inefficient for both teacher and student, requiring more student-teacher interaction, and more subjective judgement on the part of the teacher.

On the other hand, processes are inherently observable—and what can be observed can be measured or evaluated. The problem is many students (even motivated students) frequently go to great lengths to avoid documenting the work they are doing. Our research with students revealed that while they are eager to engage in challenging, meaningful learning activities, they perceive a difference between learning and documenting. Learning is fun. Writing reports, filling out worksheets, and answering questions are not fun.

IMPLICATIONS FOR BETTERAT/SCHOOL
Much of the time and effort required on the part of teachers to do meaningful process assessment could be minimized if students could organize and document their learning activities more effectively. We heard from many teachers how much they invest in preparing themselves for student conferences to make sure that no learning opportunity is missed. We also heard from both teachers and students how little students prepare for these conferences, where the right bit of feedback can change the trajectory of the student's achievements. Yet students frequently come to the table empty handed, with no record of the work they have been doing and no way to talk about the problems they are having. BetterAt/School removes the fun/not fun dichotomy in the learning process and makes the pursuit of, capture of, and reflection on learning seamless—and visible—from beginning to end.

Assessment Model

More abstract ↑

RELATED CONCEPTS

Concepts are abstractions that help us understand how things work.

**IMPOSSIBLE TO OBSERVE
EASY TO MEASURE**

Speed limit   **Cities**
                                    Geography
Small towns
              Maps
                       Gas mileage
Distances
                  GPS
Highway patrol   **Interstate highway system**

REAL LIFE

Real life is our lived experience.

**Traveling by car from
New York to St. Louis.**

PROCESSES AND PLANS

Processes and Plans are the concrete details that record how we navigate life to accomplish our goals.

**EASY TO OBSERVE
DIFFICULT TO MEASURE**

1. Map the route.
2. Determine how many miles or hours per day to drive.
3. Identify locations of motels, restaurants, and rest stops.
4. Notify friends of when I will be arriving and make reservations at motels.
5. Identify local landmarks to visit on the way.
6. Change oil in car, get tune-up, and check tires.
7. Don't get a speeding ticket.

More concrete ↓

EXAMPLE

Paul Wants to See How Students Apply What They Are Learning

Teachers like Paul understand that students possess capabilities that can't be measured on standardized tests

Paul is a science teacher in a Chicago public high school. He strives to give his students fun projects that are motivating yet closely aligned with the Illinois Learning Standards for Science. At the end of each teaching unit, Paul uses these standards to assess his students' mastery of important concepts and skills. Paul's students keep feedback logs that pinpoint their progress with each standard so that when they need to study for high-stakes exams, they know where to focus their energy.

One of Paul's favorite projects is a physics assignment that was developed by Northwestern University in which students build digital models of roller coasters using iPads he obtained through a small grant. Students love testing how their designs measure up as they learn important physics content, like the laws of energy conservation. Despite feeling good about assigning a challenging, engaging group project, Paul still struggles with assessment. His assessment rubrics are based on content knowledge, so while he can easily identify which concepts the students have mastered, he finds it difficult to evaluate each student's process. What he is really interested in knowing—how students use trial and error, how they correct their mistakes, and how they come up with new solutions—is difficult to track. He knows that for many of his students, the content they learned for the test is quickly forgotten, so it is important to be able to evaluate how well they can apply what they know.

Paul is looking for an assessment solution that makes student progress visible, one that he can customize based on the project.

Paul and his team develop concepts during BetterAt/school's Design for Learning Workshop.

What if Paul had a way to view student work in progress so he could guide students when they need it most? **What if** he had a way to evaluate his students' learning process in addition to their mastery of concepts?

BETTERAT/SCHOOL INTERFACE WILL ENABLE STUDENTS TO...
- integrate documentation of learning into the process of learning
- immediately share with others what they have accomplished in a format that is simple and accessible
- organize their activities
- accomplishments for review by teachers and mentors

CONCEPTS
The BetterAt/School Interface and Apps

Making process assessment easy

Unlike MOOCs (massive online open courses) and online textbooks, BetterAt/School won't simply change the mode of content delivery—it will make it easier for teachers (and students themselves) to assess the learning process in real time. BetterAt/School will make it easier for students to plan, execute, and, most importantly, document their learning activities, both inside and outside of school. BetterAt/School apps will make it easy for students to capture their learning wherever they are, and instantaneously sync their work with their timelines. Teachers will be able to view student timelines remotely, making it easier to provide feedback at any point in the process, thus enabling students to make each learning activity as productive as possible and simultaneously enabling teachers to clearly see how well each student is working through the learning process—and how effectively they apply what they are learning.

❶ THE TIMELINE
The BetterAt/School timeline is the record of what students have done, and what they will do next.

❷ THE STEP
The step is the basic unit of activity within a plan.

❸ SEARCH
Find other BetterAt/School challenges or users.

❹ STUDENT-CREATED CONTENT
Steps that contain student work or activities are color-coded for quick visual identification in the timeline.

❺ NOW
Divides the timeline into *records* (to the left) and *next steps* (to the right).

❻ HELP WANTED
Students post general questions and requests to their interest network.

❼ SUGGESTIONS
Peers, teachers, and experts suggest additional resources they think will be helpful.

❽ SUBSCRIBERS
Peers, teachers, and experts form interest networks made up of everyone who is participating in a particular challenge.

[Sync]

❾ DISCUSSION
Peers, teachers, and experts provide feedback about a specific piece of student work. The archived discussion can be helpful when assessing the student's learning process.

BetterAt/School iPhone Apps
With BetterAt/School apps, students can capture their work anywhere, anytime, and instantly sync it with their timelines.

BETTERAT/POEMS
Lets students snap and caption photos with a simple research framework.

BETTERAT/INSIGHT
Lets students capture 140-character research insights.

BETTERAT/BRAINSTORM
Helps students organize ideas.

BETTERAT/INTERVIEW
Lets students record interviews and add notes.

BetterAt/School iPad App and Interface

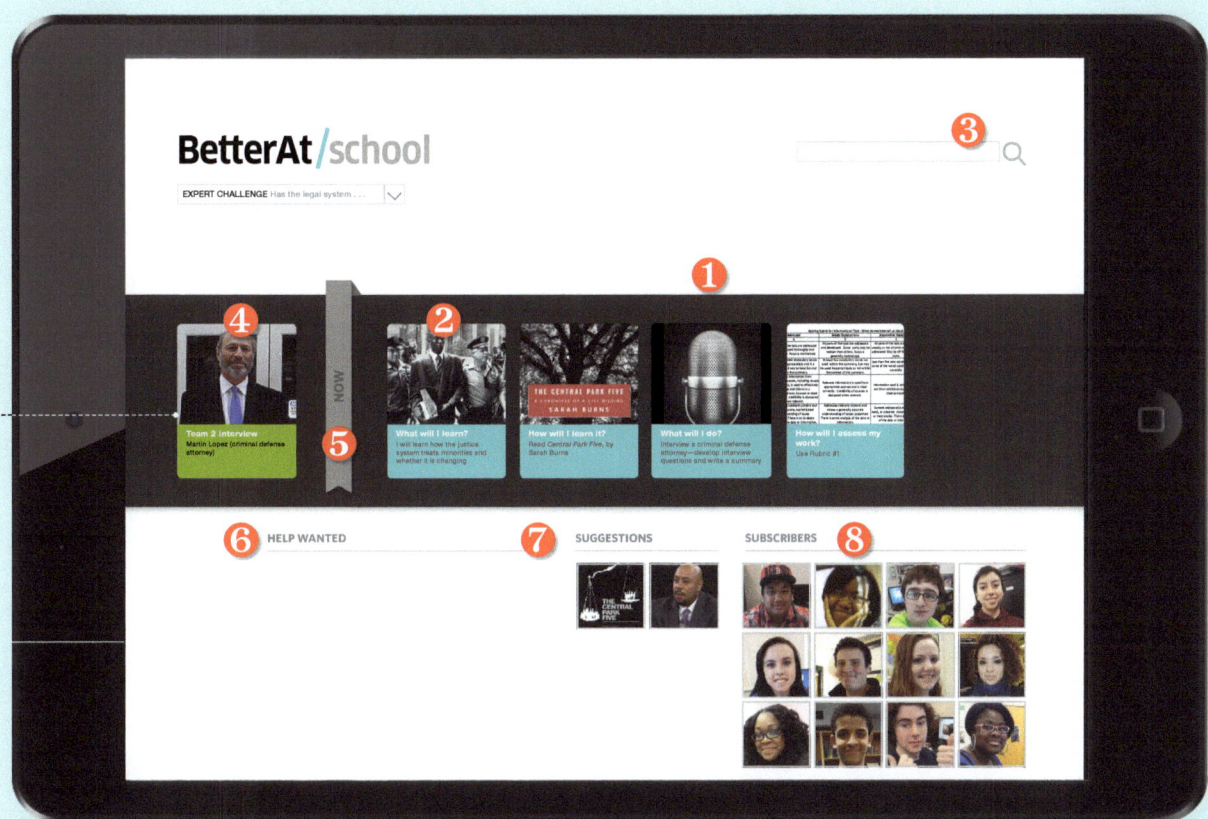
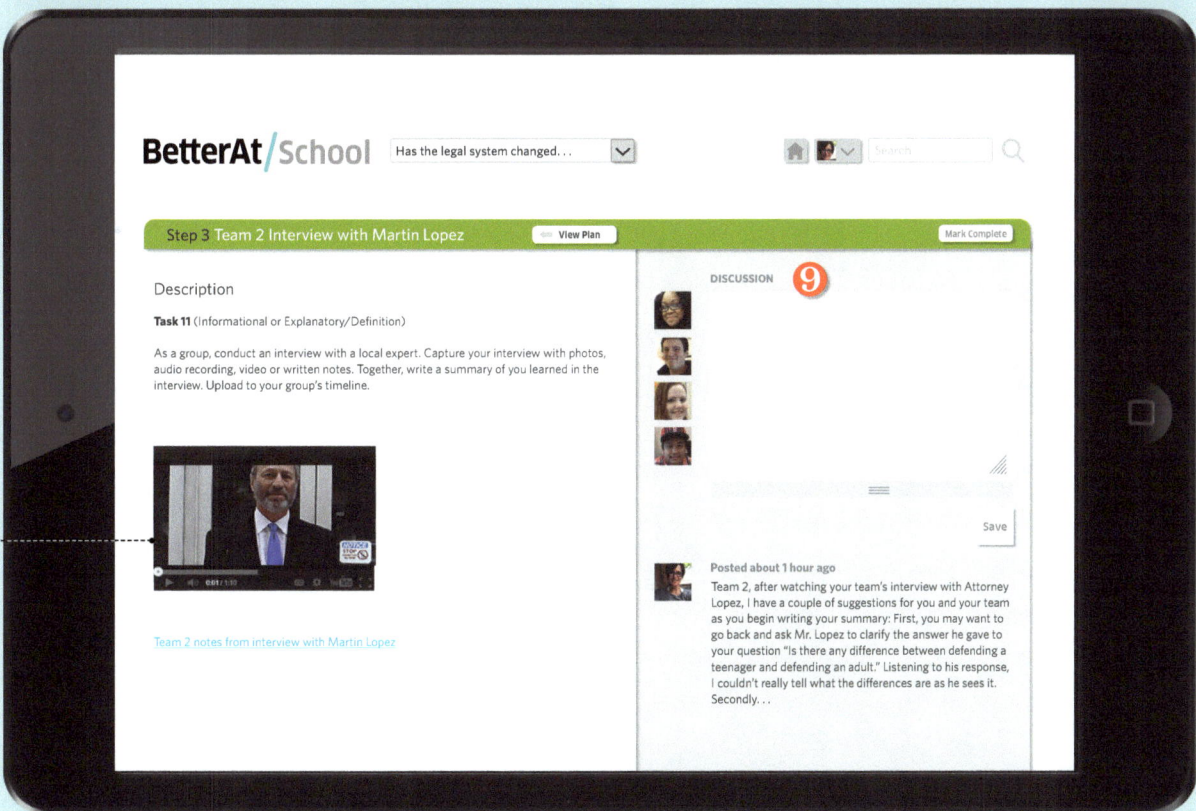

Appendix

The Design Process

The BetterAt/School research team followed a human-centered design process developed by Professor Vijay Kumar at IIT Institute of Design and focused on the objective of creating superior user experiences. The model (shown at right) encompasses seven modes: sense intent, know users, know context, frame insights, explore concepts, frame solutions, and realize offerings.

Unlike the dominant model of problem solving (below left), in which facts are gathered then solutions are brainstormed, the design process model (below right) incorporates an additional step that requires the participant to abstract the knowledge gathered from analysis. This step involves the creation of generalized models that explain phenomena in a way that fosters deeper, more sophisticated insights to emerge and a broader array of solution concepts to evolve.

MODE 1
Sense Intent

In every case, it is important to determine where to begin. Designers begin by gathering the latest information in a field, mapping trends and developments, creating overviews, and framing and reframing problems until the design team agrees on a coherent understanding of what is happening and which problem or problems to address.

WHAT WE DID
BetterAt/School began with a clear intent that evolved from previous research and was informed by the goals of the Bill and Melinda Gates Foundation: to discover meaningful ways the Common Core State Standards and best practices of interest-based learning might combine to improve both student engagement and student achievement.

The Design Process*

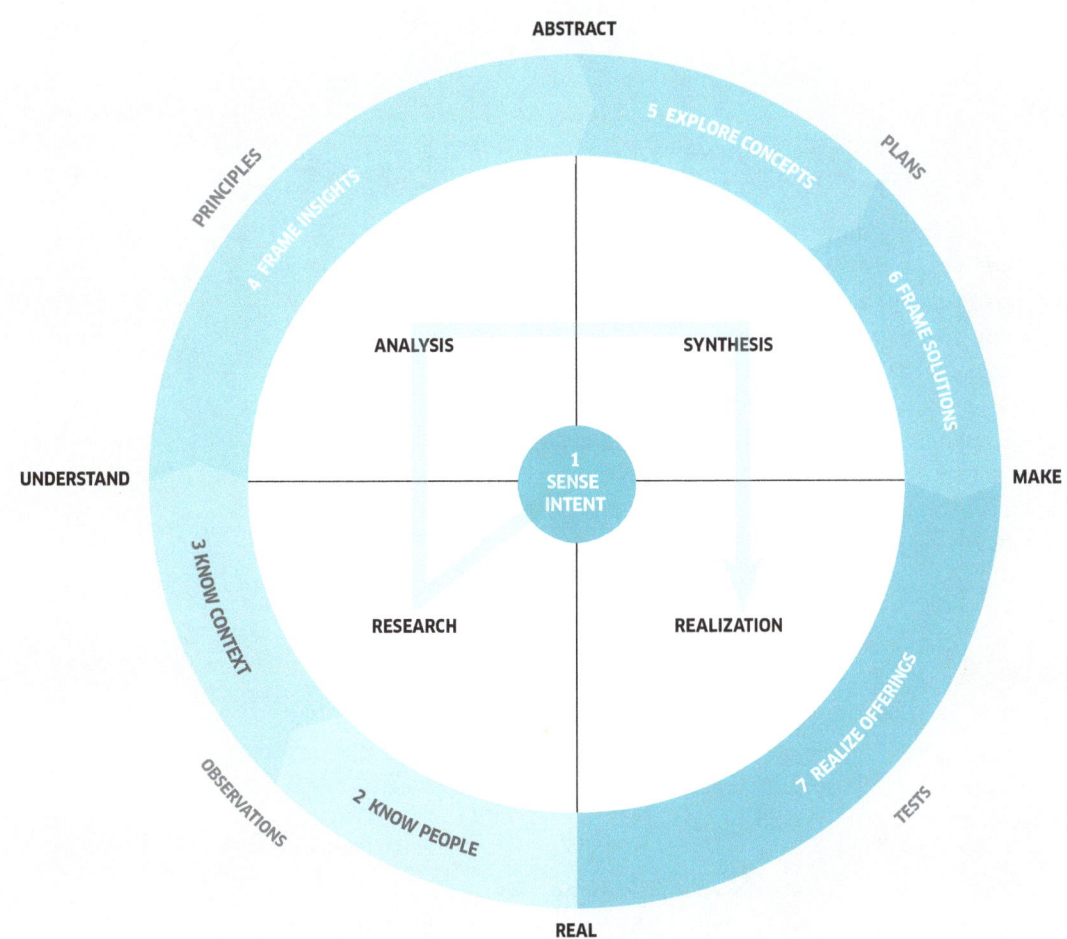

*Vijay Kumar, *101 Design Methods: A Structured Approach for Driving Innovation in Your Organization* (Hoboken: John Wiley & Sons, Inc., 2012), page 8.

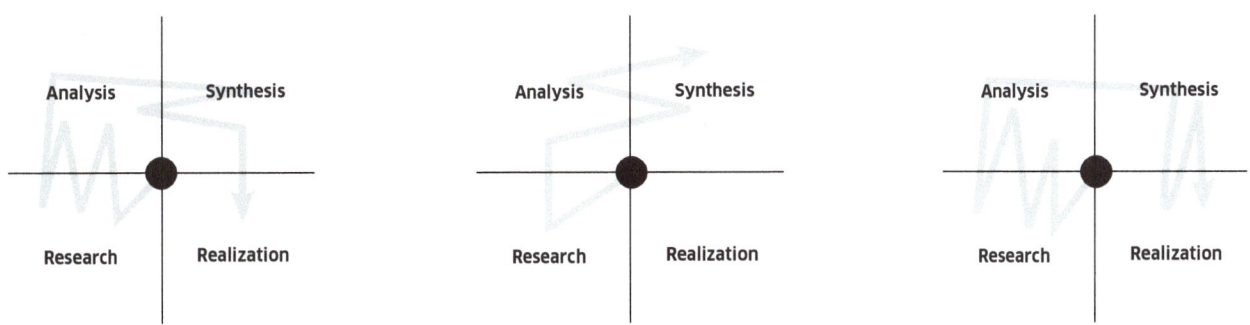

MODES 2 and 3
Know Context and Know People

The next step is to understand both the evironment in which the problem or problems exist, and the experiences shared by the end users and other stakeholders. Understanding the environment involves creating a research plan, establishing an existing knowledge base to discover emerging patterns, talking to experts, mapping the evolution of the environment, comparing the environment to other organizations, and, finally, diagnosing the conditions for innovation. Understanding people involves observing and interviewing key users and stakeholders and conducting workshops designed to explore particular findings as they emerge. Above all, the objective in this phase is to enable the design team to build insight about and empathy for the people interacting in that environment.

WHAT WE DID
In order to quickly grasp the driving issues in the debate about the value of standardized testing, expectations for Common Core State Standards, and the impact of standards on student engagement, we conducted expert interviews with individuals who could speak from direct experience working in the field, making sure we discussed the issue of standards in every school we visited and with every teacher and administrator we spoke with.

To gain insight about standards-driven classroom instruction, we visited several mainstream public schools, including very high-performing schools, where test scores were well above average, and very low-performing schools, where fewer than half the students were deemed proficient. We interviewed teachers and students in each of these schools.

To gain insight about interest-driven instruction, we immersed ourselves in two schools on the edges of the mainstream. We observed student presentations and interviewed students about where their interests come from and how they develop. We talked to teachers and administrators about the difficulties of implementing the interest-based model, tested prototypes, and spent time in organizations of informal learning. We also conducted observations and held workshops with young people participating in summer programming at youth centers in both urban centers and suburban locations.

'Advisory' at The MET

By observing how students at The MET work independently in class (known as 'advisory') and interviewing them about their internships and projects, we learned that most students struggle with knowing where to begin. Many students talked about how as freshmen they couldn't identify what they were interested in, so they relied on their teacher (advisor) to suggest options for exploring different careers. Interviews with advisors shared how difficult it often was to get students onto a career path. We learned that most students required a period of exploration (sometimes up to two years) before committing to a career goal.

Alana's internship

Alana is a junior working three days a week at the State Theater in Woonsocket, RI. Her internship requires her to assist her boss and mentor, Tom, with all aspects of setting up the auditorium—from moving pianos and speakers to setting up the sound board. By shadowing Alana and Tom as they worked, and conducting ethnographic interviews with them, the team was able to observe how a high-performing intern in action. It quickly became clear how—even for highly motivated mentors,—difficult it is for them to communicate effectively about their intern to the advisor. A small improvement in this process could dramatically improve the quality of student performance assessment.

IIT Institute of Design

The MET's Learning Through Internship (LTI) Final Exhibitions

We observed several final presentations of internship projects students had developed during the spring trimester. The presentations included structured feedback from adults and peers. Students had to learn public speaking and structure a presentation. The final submission of the work, however, was usually a huge set of binders and folders with documentation in no particular order. Not only did this require an enormous expenditure of time and effort on the student (which explains why they frequently admitted to procrastinating), but it was also tedious and time consuming for teachers to wade through in order to evaluate the work the student had done.

Thinkering Club

The objective of the Thinkering Club is to give students a chance to apply simple computer technology to solve a problem the students care about. Students identify a problem to solve and use the semester to work through the design process using Arduino, an open-source computer prototyping platform. We noticed that during the brainstorimg session, discussion of the Arduino technology did not inspire students. Only when they began looking online at examples of things other people had created using similar technology did the ideas start flowing. Seeing what they could actually DO with the technology gave the students a starting point, and discussion quickly gained momentum.

Stevensen High School

Research at Stevenson High School revealed how teachers in a high-performing mainstream public school plan their lessons. We learned that teachers will look almost anywhere for content and ideas that support their curricular goals. Teachers described searching websites, asking other teachers, and combing through shelves full of binders and folders created by themselves, other teachers or the administration. Each teacher described his or her own system for finding and saving materials, and many reported that at the beginning of their careers, this task was daunting. What was most interesting about the task of resourcing was its potential to be both tedious and frustrating yet often highly creative at the same time. Teachers seemed willing to spend a significant amount of time resourcing for two reasons: they found it creatively satisfying, and they felt the right resource had the potential to elevate an ordinary lesson to something extraordinary.

EPIC Academy

At EPIC Academy the research team observed an English class and interviewed teachers and students about how students develop interests that link to college and career. We noticed that EPIC Academy was more tightly structured than any other school we had visited—students wore uniforms, and classrooms were filled with hand-written posters reminding students of everything from the rules of grammar to rules of behavior. We heard from EPIC's career and college counselor how difficult it is to keep students focused on the college application process—figuring out where to apply, submitting their applications, writing essays, making deposits, etc. We saw that students were confident about their futures, but they also seemed overwhelmed by the need to choose a career/college path.

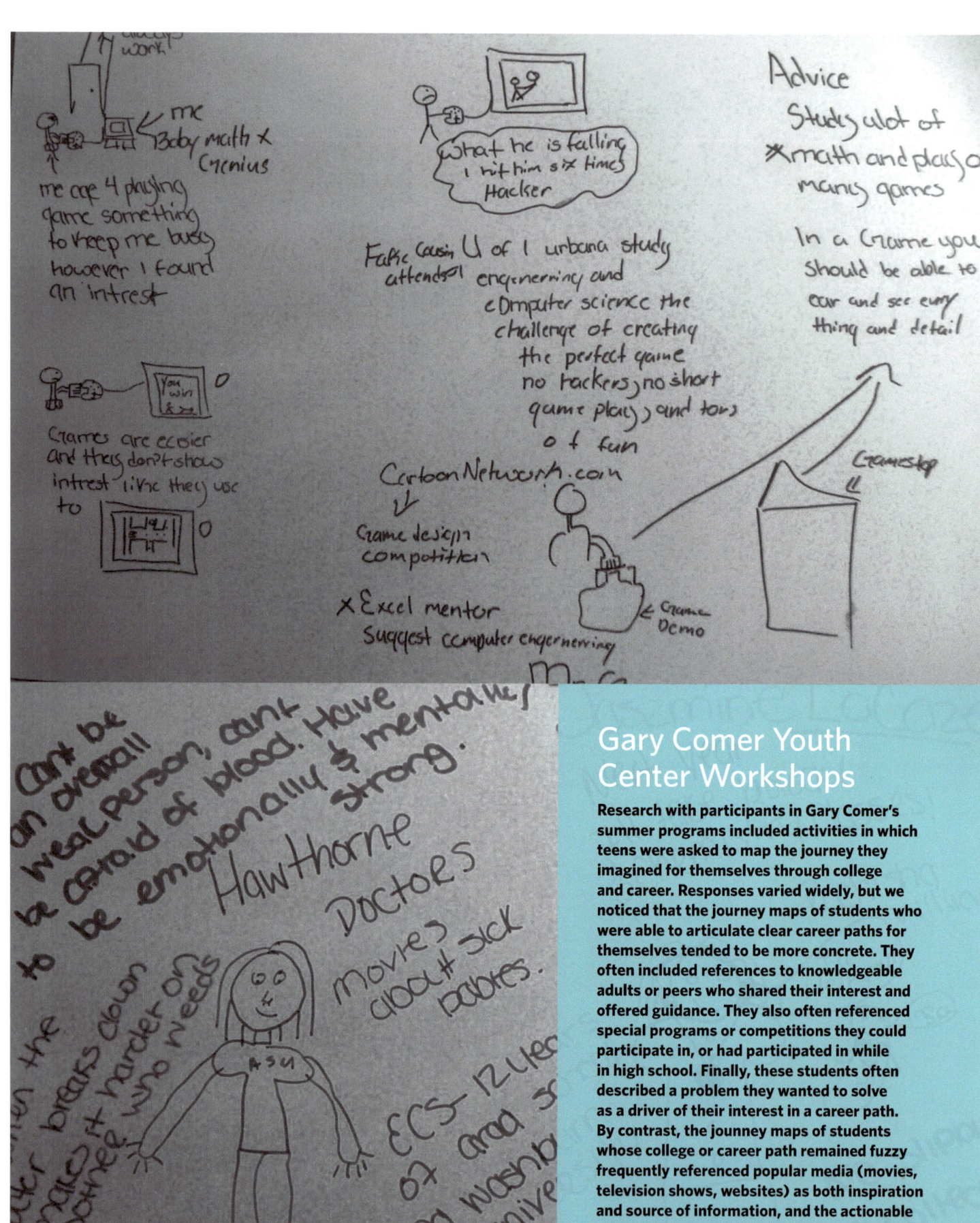

Gary Comer Youth Center Workshops

Research with participants in Gary Comer's summer programs included activities in which teens were asked to map the journey they imagined for themselves through college and career. Responses varied widely, but we noticed that the journey maps of students who were able to articulate clear career paths for themselves tended to be more concrete. They often included references to knowledgeable adults or peers who shared their interest and offered guidance. They also often referenced special programs or competitions they could participate in, or had participated in while in high school. Finally, these students often described a problem they wanted to solve as a driver of their interest in a career path. By contrast, the journey maps of students whose college or career path remained fuzzy frequently referenced popular media (movies, television shows, websites) as both inspiration and source of information, and the actionable steps these students referenced were mostly focused on courses they were taking or would soon take in school.

Bronx Guild High School

At Bronx Guild High School the team conducted contextual interviews with teachers and students, a survey of student attitudes toward assessment, and a pilot of BetterAt/School content modules. We also asked teachers to map out their teaching processes and share with us what was difficult, what was enjoyable, and what was most important to them about teaching. Their stories (and the stories told by students) revealed in highest relief the tension between a system that prioritizes standardized test performance and students' fundamental human need to find personal meaning in the process of learning. As an interest-based school, Bronx Guild works hard to maintain a student-centered culture and create a positive context for learning. Class sizes are kept small (15 to 20 students), and teachers remain with their cohort of students for the entire four years. All students are required to work in internships and to design internship projects that advance their learning. But the increasing pressure of preparing students for the New York State Regent's Exam has caused the administration to introduce a modified version of traditional subject-area instruction for all students. The experience of Bronx Guild in blending interest-based learning with traditional, curriculum-driven learning gave the BetterAt/School team confidence that a student-centered, activity-based, yet standards-driven design solution would be viable in almost any school.

While conducting the pilot at Bronx Guild, we learned that the school had just been awarded a grade of "A" from the New York City Department of Education.

MODE 4
Frame Insights

Moving to analysis mode, the team shifted out of the real world, into the abstract realm. The task of analysis is to construct meaning out of the observations gathered in research mode. The first step in this process is to look for patterns in the activities, behavior, attitudes, or mindsets of users or in the evolution of the conditions present in the context or system under study. Typically, designers do this by sorting and clustering insights in various ways in order to build up both a detailed understanding and a high-level perspective of what is happening in the problem space. In addition, we map user experiences and model the systems present in the context. In this step, the goal is to visually represent our understanding through clearly annotated diagrams. The final step is to create abstract frameworks that at a high level describe the existing state for the specific purpose of driving concept generation. The experience divide model (see page 8) is a good example of an abstract framework that describes the problem in a way that suggests multiple pathways to solutions.

WHAT WE DID
The diagram below is an example of the process of interest-based teaching practiced at the Bronx Guild. We asked twenty teachers to describe in their own words their teaching processes. Each teacher described his or her own process in very unique way. At first it was difficult to discover any patterns, or to make any generalizations at all, so the team took each teacher's process apart and

Process: Teaching at Bronx Guild High School

The team saw that teaching at Bronx Guild followed a pattern of divergent and convergent thinking that culminated in a critical moment of intense engagement between one student and one teacher. We call this critical point, 'The Moment of Truth,' and because at this juncture teacher/student interaction is especially powerful, we consider this a high-leverage design opportunity.

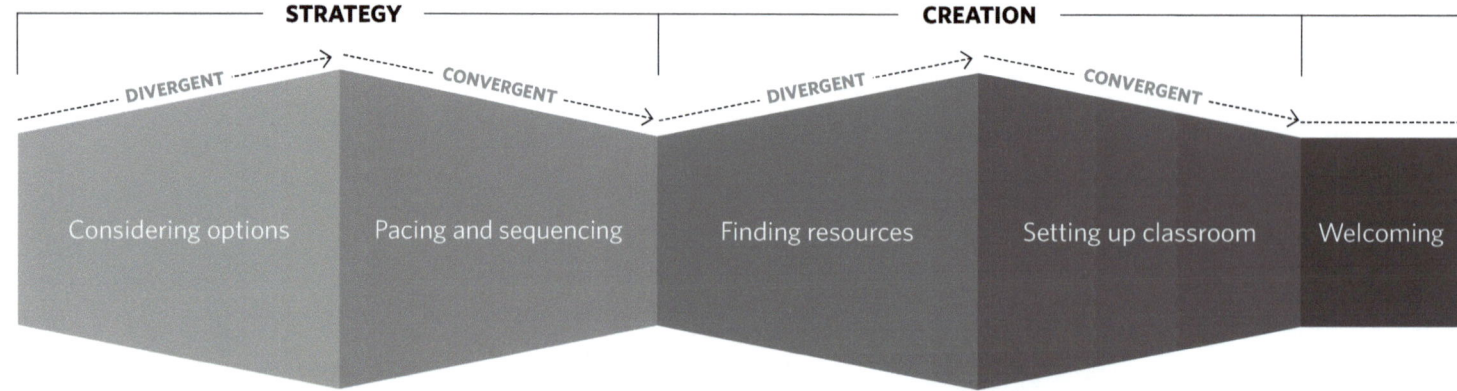

began grouping similar steps together. The result of this effort was a set of nine roughly sequential activities—considering options, pacing and sequencing, finding resources, setting up the classroom, welcoming students, sharing information, responding to students, assessing progress, and gaining perspective. In turn, these nine activities clustered naturally into four modes—strategy, creation, engagement, and reflection. Then the team plotted out the activities along a horizontal line and attempted to discern the kind of thinking—convergent or divergent*—that drove each activity. This descriptive information was overlaid on the diagram. We then refined the diagram in an effort to visually capture the pattern of convergent and divergent thinking at work in the activities.

The outcome of this work was a model that described teaching at Bronx Guild as a set of activities characterized by increasing focus that ultimately converge on a single point—the "moment of truth"—that virtually every teacher had identified as the most important step in the process, the moment when teacher and student directly engage one-to-one. Diagramming the teaching process in this way communicated the extreme fragility of that moment. We heard from teachers how easy it was to miss this opportunity, which caused a fair amount of anxiety. We also heard from students that they rarely prepared for these conferences—they admitted being prone to procrastinating, and found documenting their work to be a chore.

We realized that this might be a high-leverage design opportunity, where a small improvement at a key point in the process could lead to a disproportionate improvement in learning outcomes. We had identified the critical part of the teaching process and ascertained that it was prone to breaking down, particularly because of student resistance toward documenting their work. This insight gave the team the confidence to focus concept generation on strengthening students' ability to conference productively with teachers by finding ways to neutralize what students perceived as drudge work within the learning process.

TWO TYPES OF THINKING
Convergent thinking enables us to focus on a problem or goal and then to bring resources to bear on it. In this way, our resources converge on the problem or goal. In divergent thinking, we locate a problem or a goal and then expand our thinking about it, considering different points of view and bits of information and imagining different possibilities in order to come to a conclusion.

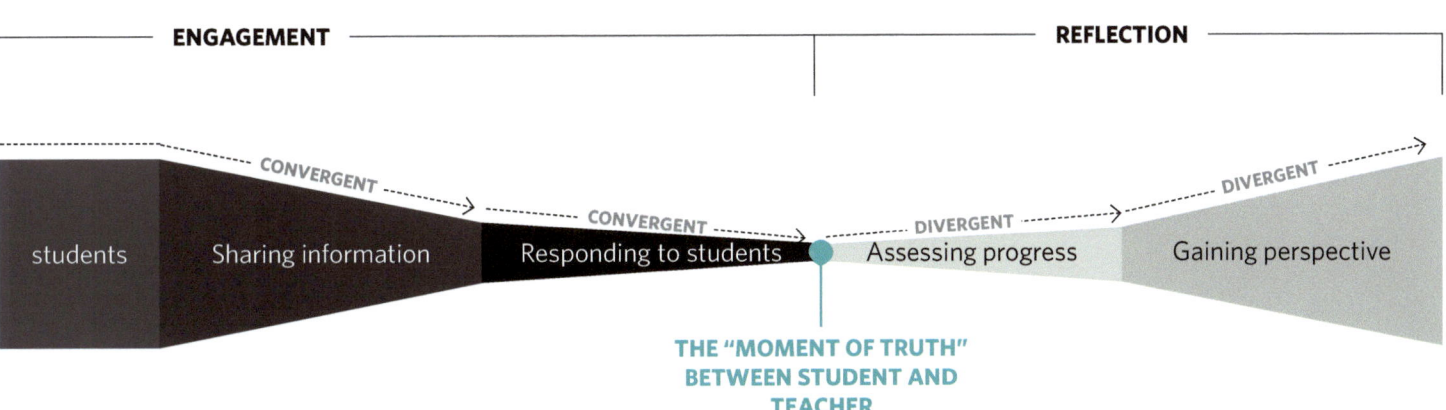

MODES 5 and 6
Explore Concepts and Frame Solutions

Exploring concepts means applying structured brainstorming activities to identify opportunities for either solving the problem or improving the conditions. This step begins by developing design principles (or design "criteria") from the insights that emerged during the analysis process. In this phase, the design team reframes assumptions made at the outset and generates hypotheses that will drive concept generation. Next, concepts are defined using the design principles and are described using sketches, diagrams, or mockups. The next step is to organize, or systematize, the concepts. The team may sort, recombine, or unbundle concepts into logical groups, documenting and archiving each iteration. Finally, concepts are shared via visualizations, sketches, prototypes, storyboards, etc., to communicate the essential value of each.

Framing solutions means systematizing individual concepts and finding ways to strengthen them by combining them with other concepts and mapping them to both business and user criteria. One way to do this is with a concept development matrix, which enables the team to see exactly which design criteria and business criteria each concept satisfies. A concept matrix is also helpful for brainstorming additional ideas to fill out the system defined by the two axes.

WHAT WE DID
Once the BetterAt/School design team understood what was happening in schools and the impact on students, teachers, and other key stakeholders, the next step was to begin imagining what the future could look like. During the synthesis phase the team began to ask questions like "What if...?" and "How can we...?"

The team began the framing solutions phase with a behavioral prototype, an exploratory mock-up designed to demonstrate what our solution will do, but not necessarily how it will do it. We also held ideation sessions with teachers from both mainstream and interest-based schools, and we tested prototypes with students in order to check assumptions and validate ideas. This highly-structured method of generating concepts and then refining, combining, and systematizing them enabled the team to more fully visualize the potential for the BetterAt/School platform.

Concept Development Matrix

BUSINESS CRITERIA

	Optimize for interest-based teachers, but also make attractive to cutting-edge mainstream teachers.	Make it easy for experts to contribute expertise.	Monetize what can be monetized in the BetterAt/School platform.	Optimize for low-income students, but also make attractive to affluent students.
Make it easy for students to capture and archive their work.	Timeline Interface BetterAt/School Apps		BetterAt/School Apps	Timeline Interface BetterAt/School Apps
Make it easy for students to connect with other students with the same interests.	Discussion Suggest Help Wanted Interest Network			
Make it easy for students to connect with adults who can mentor them.	Civic Learning Network Expert Network	Discussion Suggest Help Wanted Interest Network Civic Learning Network Expert Network	Sponsored Help Wanted	
Help students recognize how academically rigorous school work supports interesting and challenging work in the real world.	Discussion Suggest Help Wanted Activity Framework	Sponsored Competitive Challenges		Sponsored Competitive Challenges
Inspire great projects.	Starter Plans Suggest Interest network Expert Challenge Content Development Workshops	Expert Challenge Content Development Workshops	Sponsored Competitive Challenges	Sponsored Competitive Challenges
Make it easy for teachers to include process assessment in their practice.	Timeline Interface Suggest			Timeline Interface Suggest

USER CRITERIA

Behaviorial Prototyping

A behavioral prototype is a method that leverages the power of "making to learn" to refine the team's insights about user behavior and discover a starting point for the kind of high-fidelity/low-resolution prototypes to come later. In this case, the team was interested in understanding which potential features or functions of BetterAt/School were of greatest interest to teachers and how teachers might use a technology tool to replace paper lesson plans. The team constructed a simple model made of adhesive notes and butcher paper and invited a teacher to use it to plan a lesson. The running commentary of the teacher—describing how he did things, why he used or didn't use this or that feature, and what was missing—enabled the team to make judicious choices in defining a minimum viable product for piloting in schools.

Design for Learning Workshop

After conducting several rounds of research and analysis, the team invited eight teachers from both interest-based schools and curriculum-driven schools to participate in an ideation session. We created four small groups comprised of teachers and designers. They worked together to identify problems and opportunities related to project-driven learning in both kinds of schools and to distill design principles that the team could use to drive additional brainstorming.

The outcome of this workshop strengthened the team's belief that content built around modular projects, with engaging activities acting as the bridge between the Common Core State Standards and student interests, would be most appealing to both interest-based and curriculum-based teachers.

MODE 7
Realize Offerings

The first task toward realizing offerings is to identify which concepts or systems will create the greatest value for users and stakeholders. The design process begins with an intent to design purposeful solutions around peoples' lived experiences; in this final phase we revisit insights and sets of criteria (user, business, community, etc.) in order to make reasoned judgements about viable pathways forward. A key method for evaluating concepts is the building of high-fidelity prototypes for testing feasability, viability, and technical specifications. Once a portfolio of the highest-value options is assembled, implementation plans are created. The outcome of this phase is to articulate clearly how these solutions might be implemented in order to be successful. Strategy roadmaps, business models and innovation briefs help communicate to stakeholders the value of the innovation and the required actionable steps to realize it.

WHAT WE DID
A key objective for this project was to test a high-fidelity/high-resolution prototype of the BetterAt/School interface in classrooms. We began with a two-month pilot at The MET in Providence, Rhode Island. As issues and opportunities emerged from that pilot, the team made changes to the interface and revisited and refined the design strategy. During and after the initial pilot, the team conducted numerous ethnographies designed to explore more deeply some of the issues revealed by the pilot. Finally, the research phase concluded with an additional month-long pilot at Bronx Guild that tested BetterAt/School's content strategy.

In order to communicate learnings and initiate discussion about opportunity areas, we have created this innovation brief (research report), which we have organized around the three primary modes of activity in schools—learning, teaching, and assessing. Each section includes summaries of research findings related to each activity mode, and descriptions of concepts. We have also included in this appendix a step-by-step description of our process, and lists of collaborators, partners and contributors.

Our work on BetterAt/School is far from complete. In order to communicate the future strategic direction we envision, we have included a strategy roadmap (opposite) that highlights the current initiatives we are now pursuing and the near-term and medium-term initiatives we hope to pursue.

Strategy Roadmap

Current
STRATEGY Strategy is focused on technology development and the design of content frameworks.

OUTCOME Creation of a working technology platform, a suite of apps, refined content frameworks, and prototypes of content modules.

Strategic Competencies Web and app development, instructional design, design research and strategy

Near term (6 months–1 year)
Strategy Strategy is focused on service design and content development.

Outcome Platform is populated with high-quality content. Uptake among users gains momentum.

Strategic Competencies Service design, content development, marketing

Medium term (1–3 years)
Strategy Strategy is focused on development of external support networks and creation of expert-driven content.

Outcome Platform begins to achieve scale.

Strategic Competencies Program development, stakeholder development, content development, design strategy

---

Web interface — Refine interface

Content frameworks — Refine frameworks

Apps — Refine apps, market apps, expand number of apps

Starter plans — Create plans, socialize concept, refine plans, drive uptake among users

Learning design services — Design organization and service offering, market offering

Civic learning network — Design organization and programming, recruit members

Expert network — Design organization and programming, recruit members

Expert challenges — Prototype, test, drive uptake among users

IIT Institute of Design — BetterAt/School

The Research Plan

Research Areas, Research Questions, and Design Principles

We explored questions in three key areas in order to expand our view of what is involved with best practices in education—student motivation, assessing student learning, and learning with others/security. The general exploratory nature of the project was indicative of the nascent state of knowledge in the area of digital media and learning; researchers have yet to create a field theory or formulate standard frameworks and methods.

STUDENT MOTIVATION

We believe student motivation is the behavior a learner demonstrates by actively participating in his or her education with the purpose of succeeding. Student motivation (or lack thereof) is often observed through the student's tendency to attend school, arrive on time, complete assignments, participate in classroom discussions, show enthusiasm during learning activities, seek help when needed, and cooperate with peers and school staff.

Motivation is highest when teachers can relate core subjects to the interests of students, the same way motivation is high when students are learning informally about things that interest them outside of school. We believe that there is a disproportionate emphasis in schools to meet standards, rather than relating academics to interests, and that it is the low-income student who most urgently needs rich learning experience in order to remain motivated to graduate and pursue college. Our findings suggest that expert-driven learning, both formal and informal, is a best practice in high-performing schools and that lack of motivation among students in low-performing schools can be partly attributed to the absence of expert-driven learning.

ASSESSING STUDENT LEARNING

Our definition of assessment takes into account three different types that are often used together in the real world to evaluate one's knowledge or skills: self-assessment, peer assessment, and expert assessment.

Self-assessment is internal and reflective. It is most useful when trying to achieve a self-directed goal. Peer assessment happens in small groups and is helpful when trying to accomplish a shared goal. Outside, or expert, assessment is useful as feedback to gauge progress against a self-identified or shared goal or as an evaluation against a goal defined by someone else.

A good example of all three forms of assessment at work is a jazz combo that plays a nightclub. Each musician self-assesses and improves his or her playing as the set progresses. They also engage in constant peer assessment as they improvise and play off each other. The audience and the club owner provide outside assessment—the audience provides it in real time, in the form of applause or silence, and the club owner provides assessment in the form of payment and an invitation to return (or not).

Project-based learning in school is similar to the experience of playing jazz. The student is part of a group. Members work together to complete a project. Each team member must constantly self-assess and adjust his performance to keep pace with the group. Each member also assesses the other members of the group and uses the group's feedback to further adjust her performance. Teachers—much like the audience and club owner—externally evaluate the progress of the group and the outcome of the group's performance. Parents, mentors, and, in expert-driven learning,experts in the field can also externally evaluate the group's work. It is important that students experience the different modes of assessment available and learn to use them judiciously to help improve performance. Not coincidentally, this is also how we use assessment as adults working in our jobs.

LEARNING WITH OTHERS AND SECURITY

When students learn with each other and share what they are doing, learning happens in context, the way it does in the real world.

With collaborative learning and the use of technology comes the issue of online security and student safety. We believe this is a social challenge more than a technical challenge. BetterAt will provide parameters for creating closed networks, and users will use their real names as opposed to aliases.

RESEARCH QUESTIONS:
1. How do people plan lessons (kids versus teachers)?
2. How do teachers plan to motivate students?
3. How do kids create plans and connect them to standards?
4. How do teachers work in groups?
5. How do kids work in groups?
6. How do people waste or spend time?
7. How do kids get rewarded in interest-based learning?
8. How do people manage "nested" groups?
9. How are kids assessed while learning?
10. How would kids design a lesson plan with curriculum goals?
11. How do teachers do predictive planning? How do teachers do responsive planning?
12. What is an interest?
13. How are standards incorporated into lesson planning (kids versus teachers)?
14. What role do standards play outside of school?

DESIGN PRINCIPLES
Each research area provided insights which were used to create best practice models and were incorporated into the design of BetterAt/School. Out of these research areas emerged three principles to guide the vision for BetterAt/School:

1. Innovations will be found at the edges of the field, not the center.
2. Schools should be nodes on a network, not stand-alone institutions.
3. Innovations should be kid-centered, not standards-centered.

BetterAt/School Research Team
PATRICK WHITNEY
Lead investigator
Robert C. Pew Professor and Dean,
IIT Institute of Design

KEVIN DENNEY
Research Associate

ASH BHOOPATHY
Research Associate

MARILEE BOWLES-CAREY
Research Associate

LYDIA KURKJIAN
Researcher, consultant for interest-based teaching

Student Contributors
KSENIA PACHICOV
MDes 2011

EMILIA KLIMIUK
MDes 2012

REBECCA BUCK
MDes 2012

ISHAN BHALLA
MDes 2013

JARED BRYLL
MDes 2013

KAREEM HINDI
MDes 2013

Summer 2012 Research Team
LISA BLOSS
Research

GLADYS ROSA MENDOZA
Research

KRIS ANGELL
Research

MARK WESLEY
Photography, videography

MEKAEL WESLEY
Photography, videography

Digital team
XIAOFEI TANG
Web and mobile development

XIAO GREG GANG
Web and mobile development

Participating Schools

Data compiled from school, district, and city websites or the Chicago Tribune for 2012 or the last available year.

HIGH SCHOOLS

BRONX GUILD HIGH SCHOOL Bronx, NY
Bronx Guild, part of the Big Picture network, is a small interest-based public school. Students at the Bronx Guild participate in internships, project-based learning, and an advisory-style "crew" along with more traditional classes. In 2012 the Bronx Guild received a school grade of "A" from the New York City Department of Education.

Number of students: 305
Average SAT score: 1149
Graduation rate: 75.4%
Title I: Yes
English language learners: 8.22%
Special education: 28.42%
Demographics: 60.6% Hispanic, 33.6% African-American

EPIC ACADEMY Chicago, IL
EPIC Academy is a charter school on the south side of Chicago. It focuses on project-based learning that engages students in mastering skills required for college and real-world success.

Number of students: 461
Average ACT score: 16.5
Graduation rate: 61%
Title I: Yes (90.5% low income)
English language learners: 9.8%
Special education: 18.4%
Demographics: 59.4% African-American, 37.7% Hispanic

GARY AND JERRI-ANN JACOBS
HIGH TECH HIGH CHARTER SCHOOL San Diego, CA
High Tech High is an independent public charter school. Its model includes performance-based assessment, daily shared planning time for staff, state-of-the-art technical facilities for project-based learning, internships, and close ties to the high-tech workplace.

Number of students: 571
Average SAT score: 1611
Graduation rate: 99%
Title I school: No (37.1% low income)
English language learners: 9.8%
Special education: 10.9%
Demographics: 40.3% Caucasian, 27.1% Hispanic

THE METROPOLITAN REGIONAL CAREER AND TECHNICAL CENTER Providence and Newport, RI
The MET is a state-funded public alternative district of six schools operated by the Big Picture Company, a non-profit organization. The MET's individualized learning approach includes internships, individual learning plans, "advisory," and a college transition program. The MET is the model for the Big Picture network, a group of 80 interest-based schools across the country.

Number of students: 690 (district-wide)
Average SAT score: n/a
Graduation rate: 83.9%
English language learners: n/a
Special education: 16%
Subsidized free lunch: 65%
Demographics: 42% Hispanic, 27% Caucasian, 27% African-American

NOBLE STREET COLLEGE PREP Chicago, IL
Noble Street College Prep is part of the Noble Network of Charter Schools, which follows a traditional curriculum of learning and a strict discipline code to create a strong school culture. Along with its core curriculum, it offers technology, language, and sports programs that emphasize health and nutrition as well as community service.

Number of students: 599
Average ACT score: 20.6
Graduation rate: 61.2%
Title I: Yes (90.5% low income)
English language learners: 5.8%
Special education: 12%
Demographics: 83% Hispanic, 12.4% African-American

NORTHSIDE COLLEGE PREPARATORY HIGH SCHOOL
Chicago, IL
Northside College Prep is a selective, high-performing public school. Northside's offerings include its project-based colloquium program, collaboration with community and business professionals around content in every subject area, award winning extracurriculars, language programs, and study abroad.

Number of students: 1065
Average ACT score: 29.6
Graduation rate: 98.3%
Title I: No (35.4% low income)
English language learners: 0.7%
Special education: 6%.
Demographics: 41.9% Caucasian, 23.2% Hispanic

SAN DIEGO MET HIGH SCHOOL San Diego, CA
The San Diego Met is an alternative middle college high school located on the campus of San Diego Mesa College. Belonging the Big Picture network, the mission of the San Diego Met is to prepare students for college and careers through internships, project based learning, exhibitions and college courses.

Number of students: 192
Average SAT score: 1517
Graduation rate: 92.3%
Title I school: Yes
English language learners: 7.3%
Special education: 9.4%
Demographics: 46% Hispanic, 23% African-American, 20% Caucasian

SPRINGSIDE CHESTNUT HILL ACADEMY
Philadelphia, PA
Springside Chestnut Hill is a high-performing independent school. Its upper school (grade 9–12) provides students a rigorous college-preparatory program grounded in project- and passion-based learning. Along with an entrepreneurial leadership curriculum, an award-winning space, and a nationally recognized program dedicated to engineering and robotics, SCH offers a full roster of athletic and extracurricular opportunities.

Number of students: 1,100 (k-12)
Average SAT score: 1740
Graduation rate: 99%
Title I: No
Demographics: 29% students of color

ADLAI E. STEVENSON HIGH SCHOOL Lincolnshire, IL
Stevenson High School is a traditional curriculum-based school that offers more than 200 courses and has ranked in the top five worldwide in AP participation. There are 125 clubs and activities open to students. The 76-acre campus features state-of-the-art facilities including a 1,200-seat performing arts center, an Olympic-size swimming pool, college/career counseling center, tutoring centers, language labs, and a centralized technology area. Stevenson High School is the only public high school in Illinois to receive four Blue Ribbon Awards for Excellence in Education from the US Department of Education.

Number of students: 4,118
Average ACT score: 26.2
Graduation rate: 96.3%
Title I: No (4.3% from low-income households)
English language learners: 2.8%
Demographics: 70.1% White, 18.4% Asian

ELEMENTARY AND MIDDLE SCHOOLS

LEARN CHARTER ELEMENTARY SCHOOL—HUNTER PERKINS Chicago, IL
Hunter Perkins belongs to the LEARN network of college prep elementary schools serving nearly 2,300 students in grades pre-K–8th across Chicago. The schools focus on a inquiry-based, project-based workshop model. The network reports a 95% high school graduation rate and a 95% college attendance rate of alumni.

Number of students: 309
Title I: Yes (88.7% low income)
Special education: 8.7%
Demographics: 73.5% African-American, 26.5% other

NICHOLS MIDDLE SCHOOL Evanston, IL
Nichols Middle School is a traditional public middle school that emphasizes academic quality and service.

Number of students: 554
Illinois Standards Achievement Test: 87.4% or students met or exceeded standards
Demographics: 40.6% Caucasian,
27.8% African-American, 19.7% Hispanic

Participating Youth Organizations

Data compiled from organizations' websites.

GARY COMER YOUTH CENTER Chicago, IL
The Gary Comer Youth Center (GCYC) strives to provide support for all of its students to graduate from high school and prepare to pursue college and careers. GCYC offers extracurricular education in a welcoming and safe environment. Programs within the 80,000 square-foot facility include college readiness, athletics, academic tutoring, performing and visual arts, health and wellness, culinary arts, technology, media, and horticulture. The Youth Center draws its primary membership from the immediate neighborhood as well as youth from throughout the South Side.

COMMUNITY CHRISTIAN CHURCH Naperville, IL
Student Community (StuCo) is the church's ministry to students in grades 6-12. Through small groups, services, and special programming, StuCo provides environments for students to develop their Christian faith.

SOUTH SHORE DRILL TEAM Chicago, IL
South Shore Drill Team, based at the Gary Comer Youth Center, uses the performing arts to engage over 250 inner-city youth throughout their critical teenage years; mitigate the dangers of gangs, drugs, and violence; and guide members towards completing their education and becoming responsible citizens.

THE YOUTH CONNECTION Detroit, MI
The Youth Connection (TYC) is a nonprofit agency working to increase participation in after-school programs and provide year-round opportunities for youth to explore careers and develop job skills. The vision of TYC is to be the leading catalyst for change that creates sustainable improvements for the health and safety of children and youth.

References

Page 7
[1] U.S. Department of Education Institute of Education Sciences National Center for Education Statistics, Table 1 Public high school number of graduates, Averaged Freshman Graduation Rate (AFGR), and estimated first-time 9th-graders, by state or jurisdiction: School year 2009-10, http://nces.ed.gov/pubs2013/2013309/tables/table_01.asp, accessed June 22, 2013.

[2] U.S. Department of Education Institute of Education Sciences National Center for Education Statistics, Table 2. Public high school number of graduates and Averaged Freshman Graduation Rate (AFGR), by race/ethnicity and state or jurisdiction: School year 2009-10, http://nces.ed.gov/pubs2013/2013309/tables/table_02.asp accessed June 22, 2013.

[3] Balfanz, R., Bridgeland, J., Bruce, M., & Fox, J. Hornig (2013). Building a Grad Nation: Progress and Challenge in Ending the High School Dropout Epidemic - 2013 Annual Update. Washington, D.C.: Civic Enterprises, the Everyone Graduates Center at Johns Hopkins University School of Education, America's Promise Alliance, and the Alliance for Excellent Education. Retrieved from http://www.civicenterprises.net/MediaLibrary/Docs/Building-A-Grad-Nation-Report-2013_Full_v1.pdf. accessed online June 22, 2013

Page 11
[4] "Teens, Smartphones & Texting "Amanda Lenhart, , Pew Internet & American Life Project, March 19, 2012, Accessed April 9, 2013, http://www.pewinternet.org/Reports/2012/Teens-and-smartphones/Summary-of-findings.aspx

[5] "Generation M2: Media and the lives of 8- to 18-Year-Olds," Kaiser Family Foundation, 2010, accessed April 9, 2013, http://www.kff.org/entmedia/8010.cfm

Page 32
[6] Silvia, Paul J. *Exploring the Psychology of Interest*. Oxford UP: New York, 2006. Definition of interest by P.S. Wilson, Interest and Discipline in Education. London: Routledge & Kegan Paul, 1971. Quoted in Silvia, p. 196.

Page 48
[7] McTighe, J., & Ferrara, S. (1998). Assessing learning in the classroom.Washington, DC: National Education Association.

www.ingramcontent.com/pod-product-compliance
Lightning Source LLC
Chambersburg PA
CBHW042025150426
43198CB00002B/69